COFFEETIME
INDULGENCES

New-Fangled, Old-Fashioned Bread Puddings

COFFEETIME INDULGENCES

Recipes for 68 Favorite Foods That Pair Perfectly with Coffee— Morning, Noon, or Night

LINDA HEGEMAN & BARBARA HAYFORD

Illustrations by Mike Gorman

ST. MARTIN'S GRIFFIN / NEW YORK

Edited by: Barbara Anderson

Library of Congress Cataloging-in-Publication Data

Hegeman, Linda.
    Coffeetime indulgences : recipes for 68 favorite foods that pair perfectly with coffee—morning, noon, or night / Linda Hegeman and Barbara Hayford.
      p. cm.
    ISBN 0-312-13617-X
    1. Confectionery. 2. Baked products. 3. Coffee. I. Hayford, Barbara. II. Title.
    TX783.H44   1995
    641.8'65—dc20   95–31012
                                                                CIP

First St. Martin's Griffin Edition: November 1995
10 9 8 7 6 5 4 3 2 1

To our mothers and

first cooking teachers,

Icy Opal Mills and

Estelle Dorothy McGann

Love,

Linda Lou and

Barbara Jean

CONTENTS AND RECIPE INDEX

BROWNIES, BARS, AND CHEWY, GOOEY COOKIES

BISCOTTI, MANDEL BREAD, AND CRISP, CRUNCHY COOKIES

FANCY BITES, PASTRIES, AND CONFECTIONS

COZY CAKES AND PUDDINGS

PIES, TARTS, AND COBBLERS

COMPANY CAKES AND TORTES

MORE COFFEE DELIGHTS

FOREWORD

May the coffee food in this book enhance your cup of coffee.
May all your coffee bubbles collect in the center of your cup.

The Pattern of Bubbles in Coffee
and Its Weather-Forecasting Value

When you are having that first cup of coffee in the morning, you are getting not only a boost on the day but also a clue to the day's weather.

- When the bubbles in coffee collect in the center of the cup, the weather will be fair.
- When they form a ring around the edge of the cup, expect rain.
- If they scatter over the surface, the weather will be changeable.

Remarkably, this piece of weather folklore seems to work and is attributed to the way pressure affects the surface tension of the coffee. A strong brewed coffee is recommended. Instant coffee does not seem to have enough oils to create the proper surface tension.

—Bob McLain,
WRTV Meteorologist, Indianapolis, Indiana

FOOD PROFESSIONALS WHOSE RECIPES AND COFFEE THOUGHTS APPEAR IN THIS BOOK

Marcia Adams, author (*Cooking from Quilt Country; Heartland; Christmas in the Heartland; Marcia Adams' Heirloom Recipes*) and television personality (*Marcia Adams' Kitchen* PBS series)

John Ash, Culinary Director, Fetzer Valley Oaks Food and Wine Center, Hopland, California

Nancy Baggett, author (*Dream Desserts; Luscious, Low-Fat Recipes*; and *100% Pleasure*)

Dawn Bailey, Pastry Chef, Wolf Coffee Company, Santa Rosa, California

Flo Braker, author (*The Simple Art of Perfect Baking* and *Sweet Miniatures: The Art of Making Bite-Size Desserts*)

Larry Dauterive, General Manager, The New Orleans School of Cooking, New Orleans, Louisiana

Markus Färbinger, C.M.P.C., Senior Pastry Chef-Instructor, The Culinary Institute of America, Hyde Park, New York

Dave Foegley, Chef, Peter's Restaurant and Bar, Indianapolis, Indiana

Gale Gand, Chef-Proprietor, Trio, Evanston, Illinois

Susan Goss, Chef-Proprietor, Zinfandel, Chicago, Illinois

Bert Greene, the late food writer and television personality

Mary Kay Halston, Pastry Chef, Corner Bakery, Chicago, Illinois

Rita Nader Heikenfeld, CCP, food columnist, cooking instructor, radio and television personality, Cincinnati, Ohio

Bobbie E. Hinman, co-author (*Lean and Luscious Cookbook* series) and author (*The Meatless Gourmet: Favorite Recipes from Around the World*)

Patricia Jamieson (Patsy), Test Kitchen Director, *Eating Well* magazine

Steven Keneipp, CCP, Chef-Proprietor, The Classic Kitchen, Noblesville, Indiana

Stephen Lee, Proprietor, The Cookbook Cottage, Louisville, Kentucky

Edna Lewis, author and longtime Southern food expert

Alice Medrich, author (*Cocolat: Extraordinary Chocolate Desserts* and *Chocolate and the Art of Low-Fat Desserts*)

Cathy Peachey Metzger and **Martha Voigt**, Chef-Proprietor and Pastry Chef, CATH, Inc., Indianapolis, Indiana

Scott Peacock, Chef, Horseradish Grill, Atlanta, Georgia, and co-founder of The Society for the Revival and Preservation of Southern Food

Mary Etta Moose, Co-owner, Moose's, San Francisco, California

Jacques Pepin, author and television personality

Stephan Pyles, Chef-Owner, Star Canyon, Dallas, Texas

Roger J. Riccardi, Managing Director, The Culinary Institute of America at Greystone, Napa Valley, California

Eli and Leslie Richman, Owners, Oven Arts, Inc., New York, New York

John Sedlar, Chef-Proprietor, Abiquiu Restaurant, Santa Monica, California, and author (*Modern Southwest Cuisine*)

H. Patrick Snook, Director of Food and Beverage, The Kahler Plaza Hotel, Rochester, Minnesota

Marlene Sorosky, author (*Entertaining on the Run*)

Lisa Ann Straub, Pastry Chef, The Beekman 1766 Tavern, Rhinebeck, New York

Jerry A. Tewell, Pastry Chef, Square One, San Francisco, California

Jude W. Theriot, CCP, traveling cooking teacher and author (*La Meilleure de la Louisiane* and *Cajun Healthy*)

Charlie H. Trotter, Chef-Proprietor, Charlie Trotter's, Chicago, Illinois, and Las Vegas, Nevada, and author (*Charlie Trotter's*)

CELEBRATED HOME COOKS WHOSE RECIPES APPEAR IN THIS BOOK

Ruth Beyer

Pamela Bishop

Harriet Crockett

Alice Eckel

Mary Ann Grogan

Anne Hayford

Joseph Hegeman

Mary Hegeman

Sherrie Holifield

Jean Jones

Stephen Lloyd

Joanne Hayford Paulus

Midge Peschau

Jean Quinn

Anne Riley

Elaine Safrin

Bella Sokolov

Betty Stanford

Patricia Stump

Ellen Walsh

ACKNOWLEDGMENTS

Coffeetime Indulgences required a lot of help. We got it. It's more fun that way. We would like to express our gratitude to:

Our endearing, enduring husbands.

Our agent, Linda Hayes, for her loyalty, encouragement, and intelligence.

Our editor, Barbara Anderson, for her continued calm wisdom and the opportunity to admire her again.

Our late friend, Cathy Peachey Metzger, for her counsel and courage, and Norman Metzger, for sharing his memories.

Our coffee expert, Ted Lingle, Executive Director of the Specialty Coffee Association of America, and the members of the association who responded to our requests.

Our favorite food professionals, who generously demonstrated good taste and good will.

Our celebrated home cooks, who confirmed that the kitchen is still the heart of the home.

Our tasters and testers for their role in the development of the recipes: Jan Baker, Sarah Barker, Sharon Barnett, Joan Berger, Cynthia Boone, Carol Bubb, Shirley Christian, Anne Corr, Betty Darko, Sara Davenport, Alice Doughty, Joan Eich, Arden and Megan Elliott, Rosa Ellis, Pam Fiscus, Ann Frick, Bonnie Fulnecky, Phyllis Gamage, Barbara Gates, Julie Held, Eunice Hughes, Kay Ivcevich, Margo Jaqua, Betsy Kachmar, Bettie Keating, Sally Kerr, Jane Kohn, Pat LaCrosse, Eleanor Lopez, Ellen and Lesly Lorch, Lynn Lorton, Lin Maggard, Kate Marvel, Barb McLin, Pat Orner, Jane Perry, Karen Pigg, Charlie Popejoy, Carole Reeves, Sherri Reider, Diane Robinson, Lorraine Schlechte, Mary Schuster, Lana Seacott, Audrey Stehle, Mary Ruth Synder, Ruth Vignati, and Roberta Walton.

Our local weather forecaster, Bob McLain, for fair weather.

INTRODUCTION

**We love coffee and all the wonderful coffee foods
that enhance its enjoyment!**

While writing our first cookbook, *New-Fangled, Old-Fashioned Bread Pud-dings*, we started each workday with a cup of coffee and bread pudding du jour. We drank a lot of coffee and ate a lot of bread pudding.

The idea for our second cookbook, *Coffeetime Indulgences*, seemed only natural. Taking a bread pudding break, we looked for other choices to go with our cup of coffee. Since we have an affection for food, our choices seemed endless.

The search began. We went to our accumulated piles of recipes and discovered more than enough recipes to fill a book, but realized that over the years we had become very fussy.

We called Cathy Peachey Metzger, owner of CATH, Inc., Indianapolis' coffee cafés, and asked her to share her coffee knowledge. What coffee foods were popular at her cafés? How could we find out what was being served nationally? She recommended that we contact Ted Lingle, Executive Director of the Specialty Coffee Association of America. With his help, we were able to survey the association's membership to determine regional coffee food preferences. We heard from across the nation and the responses confirmed our perception about what people are eating with their coffee. We thank all the responding members, including Dalton Coffee Ltd. Espresso Cafés in New York City; Gourmet Cup Coffee in Lake Bluff, Illinois; Café Bliss in Fort Worth, Texas; Espresso Carts, Inc., in Tacoma, Washington; and Caffè Society in Laguna Beach, California.

Simultaneously, we turned to family and friends. They shared their best with us and are acknowledged in this book as our celebrated home cooks. We asked some of our favorite food professionals for help. They generously gave us their coffee thoughts and offered recipes that were their personal food choices of what to have with coffee.

1

From our collection of recipes, we selected those that we felt were good coffee company, then enthusiastically headed to the kitchen. We enlisted an army of tasters to attend monthly coffees held in our homes. Tasters sampled and critiqued our coffee food from our recently calibrated ovens. We asked them to be honest. They were mean. We listened. Tasters became testers, taking home surviving recipes to test in their own kitchens. We revised and retested, refined and retested the recipes until we were satisfied that we had met the challenge. Our final test for goodness was our honest-to-goodness husbands. Ted and Jack, once again, had the final word—unless we knew better.

We chose for *Coffeetime Indulgences* sixty-five-plus recipes that met our criteria:

- Each food must enhance a cup of coffee.
- Each food must have exceptional taste.
- Each recipe must be clear and concise.
- Each recipe must be dependable.

Coffeetime Indulgences is divided into categories of coffee food starting with breakfast cakes, morning delights, muffins, scones, and breads. Choices for midday respites include brownies, bars, biscotti, cozy cakes, puddings, crisp and gooey cookies. Evening is for fancy bites, company cakes, pies, tarts, tortes, and more. We have your time and pleasure at heart. We purposefully omitted recipes for bagels and croissants—good coffee food, but life is just too short. We have found from experience that good coffee food is to enjoy with coffee anytime, many times of the day. We invite you to take a coffee break and browse through our book. What to have with coffee is now your delicious decision.

SECRETS

PRIMARY SECRETS

- Use the best and freshest ingredients you can find.
- Organize your work area and your ingredients.
- Follow the directions, at least the first time.
- Allow enough time.
- Get someone else to clean up.
- Be confident and enjoy the process and the product.

INGREDIENTS

Flour

- Use the type of flour specified in the recipe's ingredient list. Most recipes use all-purpose (white) flour. Do not substitute.
- Measure flour accurately. Spoon flour into standard dry measuring cup until overflowing. Level off excess with the straight edge of a knife. Do not measure by dipping cup into flour. Do not tap cup.
- Recipes specify when sifting is necessary.
- When a recipe calls for "sifted flour," sift even if using presifted flour, then measure.
- When dusting pans lightly with flour, tap out excess flour.

Sugar

- Measure granulated sugar accurately in dry standard measuring cup, leveling off excess with the straight edge of a knife.
- Measure confectioners' sugar accurately. Spoon sugar into standard dry measuring cup until overflowing. Level off excess with the straight edge of a knife. Do not measure by dipping cup into sugar. Do not tap cup.

3

- Recipes specify when sifting is necessary.
- When a recipe calls for "sifted confectioners' sugar," sift first, then measure. When a recipe calls for "confectioners' sugar, sifted," measure first, then sift.
- Use the type of brown sugar, light or dark, specified in the recipe's ingredient list. Measure brown sugar accurately by packing firmly into standard dry measuring cup, level with the top edge of the cup.

Baking Powder and Baking Soda

- Use double-acting baking powder.
- Measure baking powder and baking soda accurately in standard dry measuring spoon, leveling off excess with the straight edge of a knife.
- Use the type of chemical leavener, baking powder or baking soda, specified in the recipe's ingredient list. Do not substitute.
- Store baking powder and baking soda in airtight containers away from heat.

Yeast

- Use the type of yeast specified in the recipe's ingredient list.
- Liquid temperature is important when dissolving yeast. Use a thermometer to accurately measure liquid temperature range specified in the recipe.
- Use yeast before expiration date printed on package.
- Store yeast in a cool dry place.

Butter and Margarine

- Use butter or margarine as specified in the recipe's ingredient list; any substitution will change the finished product.
- Most recipes use unsalted butter. Use lightly salted butter only when the ingredient list specifies "butter."
- When a recipe calls for butter at room temperature, the butter is no longer cold.
- Butter is cut into tablespoons for ease of handling.
- Use lightly salted margarine when the recipe's ingredient list specifies "margarine."
- Do not use fat-reduced or tub margarine or spreads.

Eggs

- Use Grade A large eggs.
- When beating egg whites, use a large, clean, dry bowl and clean, dry beaters. The whites should be at room temperature and free from contaminants and specks of egg yolk.
- There are recipes in this cookbook that call for the use of uncooked eggs. Because many persons have a concern about bacterial problems with raw eggs, caution should be taken.

Milk and Cream

- Use the type of milk specified in the recipe's ingredient list. When the ingredient list specifies "milk," use whole milk.
- Use heavy or whipping cream, not light or coffee cream.
- When whipping cream, use cold heavy or whipping cream, a chilled bowl, and chilled beaters for best results.
- Measure milk, cream, and all liquid ingredients accurately. Pour milk or cream into a glass or plastic measuring cup with a spout to the desired measurement. Read measurement at eye level.

Chocolate

- Use good-quality chocolate such as Callebaut, Valrhôna, or Lindt.
- Use the type of chocolate specified in the recipe's ingredient list.
- If a recipe calls for bittersweet chocolate, do not use unsweetened chocolate.

Coffee

- Use good-quality coffee beans and brewed coffee.
- Use good-quality instant espresso coffee powder such as Medaglia D'Oro Instant Espresso Coffee.

Vanilla and Almond Extracts

- Use pure vanilla extract and pure almond extract. Do not use artificial flavorings.

Nuts

- Use fresh nuts. Store nuts in airtight containers in the refrigerator or freezer. Some recipes direct you to toast the nuts to enhance their flavor.

Follow the instructions specified in the recipe's ingredient list; watch carefully to prevent burning.

Spices

- Freshly grated nutmeg is preferred. Use whole nutmeg and grate on a nutmeg grater or on the small-hole side of an all-purpose grater.
- For optimum flavor, spices should be stored in airtight containers away from light and heat and used within a year after purchase.

EQUIPMENT

- Use the pan size specified in the recipe. Adjust baking time if substitution is necessary.
- Use heavy-gauge aluminum baking sheets and pans.
- Temperature control varies in ovens. Know your oven and adjust accordingly. Check baking product at least 5 minutes before estimated baking time elapses.
- Power varies in electric mixers. Know your mixer and adjust speed accordingly.

SECRETS FOR PREPARING THE PERFECT CUP

(Provided by Ted R. Lingle, Executive Director of the Specialty Coffee Association of America, in Long Beach, California)

Brewing great coffee is relatively easy, if you start with all the right stuff: **great beans, good water,** and **clean equipment.** It is simply a matter of putting the recipe together in the right proportions and mixing the water and coffee together at the proper temperature and for the correct length of time. With the right ingredients, a proven recipe, and complete instructions, anyone can create the "perfect cup."

Let's take a look at the ingredients for a moment. First, we have to start with **great beans.** Simply stated, we can not pull out more flavor than Mother Nature puts in. To get a great-tasting brew, we need to start with great-tasting beans. To find your favorite beans, let your palate be your guide. Your "nose knows" which ones have the fullest and most tantalizing fragrance escaping from freshly ground beans. Your "tongue can tell" which ones have the sweetest and most intriguing tastes lingering in the brew. Let your senses be your guide in finding those beans that are perfectly suited to your palate.

Finding **good water** is more elusive. Most tap water can hardly be trusted, as it is often over-chlorinated and in some areas contains too many minerals or other compounds that interfere with the brewing process. The ideal water is found in the supermarket as "crystal fresh" drinking water. It will have no chlorine residue, and it will contain 100 to 200 ppm minerals, but no salt. If your tap water is of this quality, you are lucky. If not, consider buying bottled water for your perfect cup.

Clean equipment should be a given. Yes, it takes a little work, but it is well worth the effort. And it takes a little perseverance, too. Day after day, week after week, each time the coffee brewer is used, it needs to be cleaned before the next brew. Otherwise, coffee oils dry to form coffee "tars" that can dissolve into the freshly brewed coffee and ruin the flavor of even the best beans.

So now that you have assembled all the right elements: great beans, good water, and clean equipment, you are ready to pick the proper recipe. As any true cook will tell you, getting the proportions correct is absolutely essential. If you used 2 cups of water and 1 cup of flour instead of 2 cups of flour and 1 cup of water in baking a cake, your results would be disappointing. It's no different when selecting the proper ratio of coffee grounds to brewing water. For each 6 fluid ounces of water (the amount required for a $5\frac{1}{2}$-fluid-ounce serving), use at least 9 but less than 11 grams of ground coffee. As a close approximation, 2 rounded tablespoons will contain 9 to 11 grams of ground coffee.

Now comes the technical part: "the devil is in the details." There are three things you need to check: **time, temperature,** and **turbulence.** All three relate to the coffee brewer. And, as you would expect, the better the brewer, the better the brewing performance.

Let's start with **time.** Coffee is no different from other foods—it can be undercooked or overcooked if you pay no attention to the clock when you prepare it. With coffee, undercooking produces grassy, vegetable-like flavors, while overcooking results in bitter, astringent-like tastes. The key to obtaining optimum flavors is to match the grind (or particle size of the ground coffee) to the time the brewer takes to complete its cycle. For 2- to 4-minute brew times use a "fine" grind; for 4- to 6-minute brew times use a "drip" (medium) grind; for 6- to 8-minute brew times use a "regular" (coarse) grind. If your home brewer takes more than 8 minutes to cycle 64 fluid ounces of water over the coffee grounds, consider getting a new brewer.

Temperature is another important parameter. The water reaching the bed of coffee grounds must be at least 195°F but not more than 205°F. Simply put, if the water is not hot enough, it will leave a lot of great flavoring material behind in the bed of coffee—wonderful flavors that you should be experiencing in your cup. As strange as it may seem, this also happens if the water is too hot. If you're uncertain about the temperature of the water in your coffee brewer, get a thermometer and measure. And check the temperature periodically, at least once a year. Heating elements and thermostats corrode and wear out.

Turbulence is not so easy to measure. It's that intangible difference that causes some brewers to work better than others. Except for the foaming on the surface of the bed of coffee grounds, you can't really see the effect of turbulence as readily as you can taste it in your cup. From the coffee's view, it is the action of the water in the brew basket that lifts, separates, and tumbles each little particle of coffee so that all of the flavoring material is uniformly removed. It is the difference that separates great coffee from good coffee.

So there you have it, the blueprint for a great cup of coffee. Start with great beans, good water, and clean equipment. Select the right amount of coffee for the quantity of water being used. Match the grind to the brewing time, make sure that the water in your brewer reaches the right temperature, and check to ensure that the entire bed of coffee grounds has been uniformly wetted. Put them all together and you will have found "nirvana," your own personal heaven on earth that you will proudly share with those close to you while glibly chiding others who are still searching for their "perfect cup."

BREAKFAST CAKES AND MORNING DELIGHTS

In my family the simple act of bringing one's loved one, children, parents, or houseguests an espresso in bed to start the day has been a long-standing and wonderful tradition.

How this should be done:

1. *The kind person should quietly slip out of bed to prepare the espresso.*
2. *The recipient should remain asleep or at least fake it. To wake up or get out of bed would be a great insult to the coffee bearer.*
3. *The espresso should be brought to the bedside on a small tray complete with sugar, silver spoons, and your favorite espresso cups. You may add a biscotti or crostoli, but take care. This shouldn't be breakfast in bed; the coffee is the treat.*
4. *Gently wake the recipient, who is probably already smiling, knowing that espresso is on the way.*
5. *Sit in bed together and enjoy the coffee and the company.*
6. *On weekends, don't hesitate to return to bed after step 5.*

I encourage you to replicate this tradition in your home. A steaming espresso, a simple cookie, and perhaps a good-morning kiss will let your loved ones know that whatever sorrows or joys the coming day may bring, you will be there for them.

—Roger J. Riccardi, Managing Director,
The Culinary Institute of America at Greystone,
Napa Valley, California

BUTTERMILK BREAKFAST CAKE

This coffee cake is capped with cinnamon and crunch. An anytime winner perfect for a Christmas morning.

2 ½ cups all-purpose flour
¾   cup granulated sugar
1   cup firmly packed light brown sugar
1   teaspoon baking powder
½   teaspoon salt
1   teaspoon freshly grated nutmeg
¾   cup vegetable oil
1   cup buttermilk
1   large egg, lightly beaten
1   teaspoon baking soda
1   teaspoon ground cinnamon
½   cup chopped pecans

1. Grease a 7- by 11-inch baking pan. Preheat oven to 350°F.

2. In a large bowl, thoroughly mix together flour, granulated sugar, brown sugar, baking powder, salt, and nutmeg. Break up any brown sugar lumps. Add oil and stir until mixture is crumbly. Reserve ¾ cup crumb mixture for topping.

3. To remainder of crumb mixture, add buttermilk, egg, and baking soda. Stir batter with a sturdy wooden spoon until just combined.

4. Pour batter into prepared pan and, with the back of the spoon, smooth top.

5. *Prepare topping:* Mix cinnamon and pecans into the reserved crumb mixture. Sprinkle topping evenly over batter.

6. Bake in the middle of oven for 45 minutes or until toothpick inserted in center comes out clean.

7. Remove from oven onto a wire rack and cool for 10 minutes.

8. Cut into almost squares. Serve warm or at room temperature with a cup of coffee.

Cool remaining cake completely and cover.

YIELD: *8 to 10 servings*

NUTMEG RUB CAKE

Life should be so simple.

1½ cups all-purpose flour, less 1 tablespoon
8   tablespoons unsalted butter, cut into tablespoons
1   cup granulated sugar
½   cup buttermilk
1   large egg, lightly beaten
½   teaspoon baking soda
½   teaspoon salt
½   teaspoon freshly grated nutmeg

1. Grease a 7- by 11-inch baking pan. Preheat oven to 325°F.

2. In a medium bowl and with your fingertips, rub together flour and butter. The rubs of flour and butter should be the size of small peas. Add sugar and mix well. Reserve 1 cup plus 1 tablespoon rub mixture.

3. To remainder of rub mixture, add buttermilk, egg, baking soda, salt, and nutmeg. Stir batter with a sturdy wooden spoon until just combined.

4. Sprinkle half of the reserved rub mixture evenly on bottom of prepared pan. Pour batter over rub mixture and, with the back of the spoon, smooth carefully. Do not disturb the rubs. Top with remaining rub mixture.

5. Bake in the middle of oven for 25 to 35 minutes or until top is lightly golden and toothpick inserted in center comes out clean.

6. Remove from oven onto a wire rack and cool for 10 minutes.

7. Cut into petite almost squares. Serve warm or at room temperature with a cup of coffee.

Cool remaining cake completely and cover.

YIELD: *12 petite servings*

CINNAMON STREUSEL COFFEE CAKE

Lighten up with this version of a breakfast favorite from Nancy Baggett's *Dream Desserts, Luscious, Low-Fat Recipes* (New York: Stewart, Tabori & Chang, 1992).

Nancy shares one of her warmest coffee memories: "My mother was a good cook, but she made *great* coffee. She always said it was our wonderful well water, but when I used the same water, the result was only fair. (I never did figure out her secret, and my coffee never has come close to hers.)

"The aroma of my mother's coffee was the signal for us to begin the day. Since a coal furnace provided the heat for our old farmhouse, drinking coffee was the best way to keep warm until the fire got going each morning. For many weekend breakfasts my mother also baked sweet buns or cinnamon coffee cake—which not only scented but heated the kitchen. More than thirty years later those frosty mornings with steaming coffee and fresh-from-the-oven streusel cake remain incredibly vivid in my mind."

NOTES

❏ *To reheat, cover with aluminum foil and warm in a 325°F oven for about 20 minutes.*
❏ *Cake is best when fresh, but will keep for 24 hours.*

STREUSEL

¼ cup all-purpose flour
¼ cup firmly packed light or dark brown sugar
2 tablespoons granulated sugar
½ teaspoon ground cinnamon
1½ tablespoons unsalted butter, cold
2 teaspoons canola or safflower oil

CAKE

⅔ cup coarsely chopped dark, seedless raisins
2 tablespoons dark rum (or substitute orange juice, if preferred)
2 cups all-purpose flour
1½ teaspoons baking powder
¾ teaspoon baking soda
¼ teaspoon salt
1¼ cups nonfat vanilla yogurt
⅓ cup granulated sugar
¼ cup firmly packed light or dark brown sugar
1 large egg
2 large egg whites
½ teaspoon ground cinnamon

2 teaspoons pure vanilla extract

3½ tablespoons canola or safflower oil

1. Generously grease a 7- by 11-inch flat baking pan. Preheat oven to 350°F.

2. *Prepare streusel:* In a medium bowl, stir together flour, brown sugar, granulated sugar, and cinnamon. Cut butter and oil into flour mixture, using a pastry blender, forks, or your fingertips, until mixture is crumbly.

3. *Prepare cake:* In a small bowl, combine raisins and rum and set aside to soak for 15 minutes.

4. In a large bowl, thoroughly stir together flour, baking powder, baking soda, and salt.

5. In another large bowl, using a wire whisk or fork, whisk together yogurt, granulated sugar, brown sugar, egg, egg whites, cinnamon, vanilla, and oil, until well blended.

6. With a large wooden spoon, stir yogurt mixture and rum-raisin mixture into flour mixture, until just thoroughly blended but not overmixed.

7. Turn out batter into prepared pan. Sprinkle streusel evenly over batter.

8. Bake in the middle of oven for 30 to 35 minutes or until tinged with brown and toothpick inserted in the thickest part comes out clean.

9. Remove from oven onto a wire rack and cool for at least 10 minutes.

10. Serve warm with a cup of coffee.

Cool remaining cake completely and cover.

YIELD: *8 to 10 servings*

LEMON YOGURT BUNDT CAKE

NOTES

❑ *Do not mix lemon juice and vanilla together with egg yolks; acid from lemon juice will cook yolks.*
❑ *The egg whites should be at room temperature and free from contaminants and specks of egg yolk.*
❑ *Serve with drunken berries, which are berries soaked in your favorite liqueur and topped with yogurt cheese whipped cream. This tangy whipped cream is made with equal parts of yogurt cheese and heavy or whipping cream. Yogurt cheese is easily made by placing yogurt in a cheesecloth-lined strainer and letting it drain until it loses most of its liquid. Fold yogurt cheese into whipped cream.*

Perk up your cup of coffee with this rum-soaked, citrus-glazed, fresh-tasting cake. This recipe is offered by Mary Kay Halston, pastry chef of the Corner Bakery in Chicago, Illinois, and is adapted from a recipe given to her by Jonathon Fox, chef-partner of Papagus Greek Taverna in Chicago.

"My favorite cup of coffee," Mary Kay called to say, "is the one I have when sitting down."

C A K E

4³⁄₄ cups sifted cake flour
1³⁄₄ teaspoons baking powder
³⁄₄ teaspoon baking soda
¹⁄₈ teaspoon salt
1 cup unsalted butter, room temperature, cut into tablespoons
1²⁄₃ cups granulated sugar
Grated zest of 2 lemons
1 tablespoon fresh lemon juice
1 tablespoon plus 1 teaspoon pure vanilla extract, preferably Tahitian
3 large egg yolks
1¹⁄₂ cups Dannon plain premium yogurt
3 large egg whites, room temperature
¹⁄₃ cup plus 2 tablespoons granulated sugar

S Y R U P

1 cup water
1¹⁄₂ cups granulated sugar
¹⁄₂ cup dark rum

G L A Z E

2 cups sifted confectioners' sugar
2 tablespoons fresh lemon juice
2 tablespoons heavy or whipping cream
Confectioners' sugar, enough to dust top of cake

1. Brush a 12-cup Bundt pan with melted butter and dust lightly with flour. Be sure to tap mold upside down to release all loose flour. Preheat oven to 325°F.

14

2. Sift together sifted cake flour, baking powder, baking soda, and salt. Set aside.

3. In a large bowl and with an electric mixer set on medium speed, use whip attachment to cream butter and the 1⅔ cups granulated sugar with zest until light and fluffy and doubled in volume. Beat in lemon juice and vanilla until thoroughly combined. Gradually beat in egg yolks. Stop mixer and scrape down bottom and sides of bowl as necessary. Fold in yogurt by hand.

4. In a large, clean, dry bowl and with an electric mixer set on high speed, whip egg whites with the ⅓ cup plus 2 tablespoons granulated sugar until meringue-like and quadrupled in volume. With a rubber spatula, gently fold first egg whites, then sifted dry ingredients, into yogurt mixture. Make sure no pockets of flour remain.

5. Pour batter into prepared pan and, with the back of the rubber spatula, gently smooth top.

6. Bake in the middle of oven for 1 hour or until cake tester inserted in center comes out clean.

7. Prepare syrup and glaze while cake is baking.

8. *Prepare syrup:* In a thick-bottomed sauce pot, combine water, sugar, and rum. Cook over medium heat until reduced by half. Remove from heat.

9. *Prepare glaze:* In a medium bowl, whisk together sifted confectioners' sugar and lemon juice until smooth. Slowly add just enough cream so that glaze has a medium-thick consistency. If glaze is too thick, it will not run smoothly. If glaze is too thin, it will soak into cake.

10. Remove cake from oven onto a wire rack and allow to rest in pan for 10 minutes. Pierce cake, 30 times or so, with a long, thin skewer. Slowly pour syrup over cake. The syrup may still be warm. Let cake rest in pan for 1 hour.

11. Turn out cake onto a serving plate. Some syrup may run out. When cake is cool, drizzle with glaze, as much or as little as you like. Dust with confectioners' sugar when glaze is set.

12. Cut into slices. Serve at room temperature with a cup of coffee.

Cover remaining cake.

YIELD: *12 servings*

MRS. JOHNSON'S COFFEE COFFEE CAKE

Bert Greene, the late food writer and television personality, developed this recipe, which he described as "a prodigious golden Bundt, thick with brown sugar and stuffed to the crumbs with chopped walnuts and currants."

Bert reminisced, "Mrs. Johnson's fabled coffee cake is a confection it took me half a lifetime to get right. A reconstruction of a childhood memory is a will-o'-the-wisp effort at best—yet when the scent of this cake baking in an oven assails my nostrils, the past is recaptured faster than you could eat a madeleine!"

NOTE

❏ *We used Medaglia D'Oro Instant Espresso Coffee powder. We dissolved 1 teaspoon instant espresso coffee powder in 1 tablespoon hot water for each tablespoon of strong coffee.*

CAKE

2	cups sifted all-purpose flour
1	teaspoon baking powder
1	teaspoon baking soda
1/8	teaspoon salt
8	tablespoons unsalted butter, room temperature
1 1/4	cups granulated sugar
2	large eggs
1	tablespoon strong coffee
1/2	teaspoon pure vanilla extract
1 1/4	cups sour cream

FILLING

1/4	cup currants, soaked in hot water to cover for 8 to 10 minutes, drained
1/2	cup firmly packed dark brown sugar
1/3	cup finely chopped walnuts
2	teaspoons ground cinnamon
2	teaspoons instant coffee powder

COFFEE GLAZE

1	cup confectioners' sugar
3	tablespoons strong coffee
1/2	teaspoon half-and-half
1/4	teaspoon pure vanilla extract

1. Generously butter bottom and sides of a 12-cup Bundt pan or 10-cup tube pan.

16

2. Thoroughly mix together sifted flour, baking powder, baking soda, and salt. Set aside.

3. In a large bowl and with an electric mixer set on medium speed, cream together butter and granulated sugar until light and fluffy. Add eggs, one at a time, beating well after each addition. Beat in coffee and vanilla until thoroughly combined.

4. Reduce mixer speed to low. Add flour mixture alternately with sour cream, beating well after each addition, beginning and ending with flour mixture. Stop mixer and scrape down bottom and sides of bowl as necessary. Reserve.

5. Preheat oven to 375°F.

6. *Prepare filling:* In a small bowl, combine drained currants, brown sugar, walnuts, cinnamon, and coffee powder.

7. Spread a fourth of the reserved batter into bottom of prepared pan. Sprinkle with a third of the filling. Repeat layering twice, ending with batter.

8. Bake in the middle of oven for 55 to 60 minutes or until cake tester inserted in center comes out clean.

9. Remove from oven onto a wire rack and cool in pan for 20 minutes. Remove cake from pan onto wire rack and cool completely.

10. *Prepare glaze:* In a small bowl, whisk together the confectioners' sugar, coffee, half-and-half, and vanilla until smooth and creamy.

11. Spoon glaze over cake. Let glaze set.

12. Cut into slices. Serve at room temperature with a cup of coffee.

Cover remaining cake.

YIELD: *12 servings*

ORANGE PECAN STICKY BUNS

Rise to the occasion with this sweet dream to prepare. The yeast dough and rich caramel topping are flavored with zesty orange. What a way to wake up!

SWEET DOUGH
1 cup all-purpose flour
½ cup granulated sugar
1 ¼-ounce package rapid-rise active dry yeast
½ teaspoon salt
Grated zest of ½ orange
¾ cup milk
¼ cup water
8 tablespoons unsalted butter, cut into tablespoons
1 large egg, lightly beaten
2½ cups all-purpose flour, divided
Additional all-purpose flour, enough to knead dough, up to ½ cup

CINNAMON FILLING
½ cup granulated sugar
½ cup chopped pecans
1½ teaspoons ground cinnamon
4 tablespoons unsalted butter, melted

ORANGE TOPPING
1½ cups granulated sugar
1 cup heavy or whipping cream
¼ cup fresh orange juice
8 tablespoons unsalted butter, cut into tablespoons

1. In a large bowl, thoroughly mix together the 1 cup flour, ½ cup sugar, yeast, salt, and zest. Set aside.

2. In a heavy medium saucepan, combine milk, water, and butter. Over low heat, cook until very warm, 120–130°F. Butter does not need to melt. Remove from heat.

3. With an electric mixer set on low speed, gradually add warm milk mixture to flour mixture. Increase mixer speed to medium and beat for 2 minutes. Stop mixer and scrape down bottom and sides of bowl as necessary.

4. Reduce mixer speed to low. Add egg and ¾ cup of the 2½ cups flour and beat for 2 minutes, scraping bowl as necessary. With a sturdy wooden spoon, stir in enough of the remaining 1¾ cups flour to make a soft dough.

5. On a lightly floured wooden board, knead dough until smooth and elastic, 10 minutes. Add additional flour as needed to keep dough from sticking to board; do not add any more flour than necessary and no more than ½ cup. Shape dough into a ball.

6. In a large buttered bowl, turn dough until it is completely coated with butter. Loosely cover bowl first with plastic wrap, then with a clean dish towel. Refrigerate several hours or overnight.

7. Punch down dough. Turn out onto a lightly floured wooden board and cut into two equal portions. Cover with the dish towel and let rest for 15 minutes.

8. *Prepare filling:* In a small bowl, combine sugar, pecans, and cinnamon.

9. Generously butter two 9-inch round cake pans.

10. On the lightly floured wooden board, roll one portion of the dough into a 16- by 12-inch rectangle. Brush with half of the melted butter. Sprinkle with half of the filling. Starting at the 16-inch side, snugly roll dough, jelly-roll fashion, and pinch seam to seal. Cut roll into 10 equal pieces, each about 1½ inches.

11. Place buns, cut side down, 1½ inches apart, into prepared pan and cover with a clean dish towel. Let rise in warm place until doubled, 1 hour. Buns will continue to rise in oven. Repeat with remaining dough.

12. Ten minutes before baking, preheat oven to 350°F.

13. *Prepare topping:* In a heavy, medium saucepan, combine sugar, cream, orange juice, and butter. Over medium heat, bring to a boil, stirring occasionally. Boil for 3 minutes. Pour topping over buns.

14. Bake in the middle of oven for 35 minutes or until golden brown and the topping is caramelized and bubbles up from bottom.

15. Remove from oven onto a wire rack and cool in pan for 1 minute. Generously butter enough aluminum foil to lay out all the buns. Remove buns from pans as soon as the caramel topping begins to harden. Carefully turn out onto the buttered foil, releasing buns and syrup, and cool for at least 10 minutes.

16. Serve warm with a cup of coffee.

Cool remaining buns completely and cover.

YIELD: *20 buns*

SOPAIPILLAS

This recipe for pillow-like doughnuts was developed by John Sedlar, chef-proprietor of Abiquiu Restaurant in Santa Monica and San Francisco, California, for his cookbook, *Modern Southwestern Cuisine* (Ten Speed Press: Berkeley, California). Chef Sedlar explains, "The sopaipilla is the doughnut of the Southwest. Sometimes I eat them plain with powdered sugar or cinnamon sugar, but usually I pile on gobs of chile preserves that I can in the fall when chiles are at their sweetest and ripest."

NOTES

❑ *Sopaipillas may be served with honey flavored with red chile flakes or sage.*
❑ *We rolled out the dough a little thinner than ¼ inch to yield 20 to 24 sopaipillas. If dough is rolled too thin, sopaipillas will not puff up.*
❑ *We generously dusted the sopaipillas with confectioners' sugar.*

2	**cups all-purpose flour**
2	**tablespoons baking powder**
1	**teaspoon salt**
1	**teaspoon lard or shortening**
1	**cup steaming milk**
½	**cup all-purpose flour**
	Vegetable oil, for deep frying

1. In a large mixing bowl, stir together the 2 cups flour, baking powder, and salt. Add lard or shortening and rub it into dry ingredients with your fingertips.

2. Add milk and work it in by hand. Gradually add enough of the ½ cup flour to make a soft but dry dough that comes away from the bowl and can be gathered together in a ball.

3. On a lightly floured wooden board, knead the dough for a few minutes until smooth. Cover dough with a clean kitchen towel and let it rest for about 45 minutes.

4. On the lightly floured wooden board, roll dough with your hands into an even rope, about 1 inch thick. Cut rope in half.

5. Keeping board lightly floured, roll out half of the rope with a rolling pin to make a long rectangle about ¼ inch thick and 3 inches wide. With a long, sharp knife, cut rectangle into triangles with sides about 4 inches long. Place triangles in single layers between sheets of wax paper. Repeat with remaining half of rope.

6. Heat several inches of oil in a deep-fat fryer or large heavy skillet to a temperature of 375°F.

7. Drop triangles of dough, a few at a time, into hot oil. They will sink to the bottom, then gradually rise to the surface. Keep pushing them under with a slotted spoon or wire skimmer as they gradually puff up. Fry them for 1 to 1½ minutes, turning them once, until golden.

8. Drain on paper towel.

9. Serve hot on individual plates or in a towel-lined basket with chile preserves and a cup of coffee.

YIELD: *20 to 24 sopaipillas*

MUFFINS AND SCONES

As for me, a day without coffee is a day without sunshine. It is the most comforting drink for me. Otherwise, I will have a violent headache.

—Edna Lewis, author and long-time Southern food expert

BANANA BRAN MUFFINS

Cathy Peachey Metzger, the late chef-proprietor, and Martha Voigt, pastry chef, of CATH, Inc., in Indianapolis, Indiana, developed this recipe for a naturally moist and addictive muffin.

Martha remembers Cathy saying, "When I am home, taking time off from work, I start to think about the Banana Bran Muffins and just have to get in the car, go down, and get one."

NOTES

❑ *Freeze ripe bananas in their skins; defrost and mash as needed.*
❑ *We filled paper cups generously with batter because these muffins will not rise significantly.*

1   large egg
¾   cup firmly packed light brown sugar
1⅓ cups well-mashed very ripe bananas (4 medium)
⅓   cup vegetable oil
1   teaspoon pure vanilla extract
1½ cups all-purpose flour
½   cup unprocessed wheat bran (millers bran)
½   cup chopped walnuts
2   teaspoons baking powder
½   teaspoon baking soda
¼   teaspoon salt
1   teaspoon ground cinnamon

1. Line a 12-cup standard muffin pan with paper baking cups. Preheat oven to 375°F.

2. In a medium bowl and with a sturdy wooden spoon, beat egg and sugar until smooth. Beat in bananas, oil, and vanilla. Let stand for a minute.

3. In a large bowl, thoroughly mix together flour, wheat bran, walnuts, baking powder, baking soda, salt, and cinnamon. With the spoon or a rubber spatula, fold banana mixture into flour mixture until dry ingredients are just moistened and no pockets of flour remain.

4. Scoop approximately ¼ cup batter into each muffin cup.

5. Bake in the middle of oven for 20 minutes or until toothpick inserted in center comes out clean.

6. Remove from oven and turn out muffins onto a wire rack. Cool for 10 minutes.

7. Serve warm or at room temperature with a cup of coffee.

Cool remaining muffins completely and cover.

YIELD: *12 muffins*

ROSEMARY MUFFINS

Stephen Lee, proprietor of The Cookbook Cottage in Louisville, Kentucky, shares his recipe for this slightly sweet, rosemary-scented muffin.

Stephen says, "There is no greater joy than to savor my first cup of morning coffee, sitting on a stone in my summer herb garden—the quiet, the smells, the coffee."

¾   **cup milk**
½   **cup raisins**
1   **tablespoon finely chopped fresh rosemary**
4   **tablespoons unsalted butter, cut into tablespoons**
1   **large egg**
1½ **cups all-purpose flour**
¼   **cup finely chopped pecans, toasted in a 350°F oven for 6 to 8 minutes**
½   **cup granulated sugar**
2   **teaspoons baking powder**
¼   **teaspoon salt**

1. Line a 12-cup standard muffin pan with paper baking cups. Preheat oven to 350°F.

2. In a small heavy saucepan over medium heat, simmer milk, raisins, and rosemary for several minutes. Remove from heat, add butter, and stir until butter is melted. Cool. Whisk egg into cooled milk mixture.

3. In a large bowl, thoroughly mix together flour, pecans, sugar, baking powder, and salt. With a sturdy wooden spoon, stir milk mixture into flour mixture until dry ingredients are just moistened and no pockets of flour remain.

4. Spoon batter into prepared muffin cups, filling each one about ⅔ full.

5. Bake in the middle of oven for 20 minutes or until lightly golden and toothpick inserted in center comes out clean.

6. Remove from oven and turn out muffins onto a wire rack. Cool for 10 minutes.

7. Serve warm or at room temperature with a cup of coffee.

Cool remaining muffins completely and cover.

YIELD: *12 muffins*

ORANGE-DATE PUMPKIN MUFFINS

Patsy Jamieson, test kitchen director of *Eating Well* magazine, created this recipe for a nutrient-packed muffin.

Patsy tells us, "I go out of my way to seek out good coffee: freshly roasted beans—perhaps La Minita from Terazu in Costa Rica—carefully brewed and served in a bowl topped with steamed milk. It sets the tone for the entire day."

(Reprinted by permission of *Eating Well, The Magazine of Food & Health,* © 1995.)

NOTE

❑ *We filled paper cups generously with batter because these muffins will not rise significantly.*

1½ **cups all-purpose white flour**
½ **cup whole-wheat flour**
2 **teaspoons baking powder**
1 **teaspoon baking soda**
1 **teaspoon salt**
½ **teaspoon ground cinnamon**
1 **large seedless orange, unpeeled with stem removed, well scrubbed and cut into 8 sections**
1 **large egg**
1 **large egg white**
⅔ **cup pumpkin purée**
½ **cup firmly packed light brown sugar**
¼ **cup honey or light corn syrup**
3 **tablespoons vegetable oil, preferably canola oil**
¾ **cup chopped dates**
3 **tablespoons chopped walnuts or pecans**

1. Line a 12-cup standard muffin pan with paper baking cups or spray with nonstick cooking spray. Preheat oven to 400°F.

2. In a large bowl, whisk together flours, baking powder, baking soda, salt, and cinnamon. Set aside.

3. Place unpeeled orange sections in a food processor and puree. Add egg, egg white, pumpkin, sugar, honey or corn syrup, and oil; process until mixed in. Stop processor and scrape down sides of work bowl as necessary.

4. Make a well in center of dry ingredients and add orange mixture and dates; stir with a rubber spatula to just moisten dry ingredients.

5. Spoon batter into prepared muffin cups and sprinkle with nuts.

26

6. Bake in the middle of oven for 18 to 20 minutes or until the tops spring back when touched lightly.

7. Remove from oven and turn out muffins onto a wire rack. Cool for 10 minutes.

8. Serve warm or at room temperature with a cup of coffee.

Cool remaining muffins completely and cover.

YIELD: *12 muffins*

GRANDPA'S CANADIAN SCONES

Honest-to-goodness goodness. A lovely, plain sugared scone that is soon to become an American favorite.

NOTE

❑ *These scones should be moist. Take care not to overbake.*

2   **cups all-purpose flour**
1/3   **cup granulated sugar**
1   **tablespoon baking powder**
1/2   **teaspoon salt**
1/2   **cup solid shortening**
1/2   **cup milk**
1   **large egg**
2   **tablespoons unsalted butter, very soft**
1   **tablespoon granulated sugar**

1. Line a baking sheet with parchment paper. Preheat oven to 450°F.

2. In a large bowl, sift together flour, the 1/3 cup sugar, baking powder, and salt. With a wire pastry blender or a fork, cut shortening into flour mixture until shortening is completely coated with flour and mixture resembles coarse crumbs.

3. Beat together milk and egg. Reserve 2 tablespoons of milk mixture to brush tops of scones. Add remaining milk mixture to flour mixture and, with a fork, stir until blended.

4. On a lightly floured wooden board, knead dough for a few seconds. Roll out dough into a 9-inch square, 3/8 inch thick. Cut dough into 3-inch squares. Spread squares evenly with butter and fold corner to corner to form triangles. To get 10 scones, rework dough scraps. Brush tops of scones with reserved milk mixture and sprinkle with the 1 tablespoon sugar.

5. Place scones, 2 inches apart, on parchment-lined baking sheet.

6. Bake in the middle of oven for 8 to 10 minutes or until golden brown.

7. Remove from oven onto a wire rack and cool for 5 minutes.

8. Serve warm with a cup of coffee.

Cool remaining scones completely and cover.

YIELD: *10 scones*

REAL ENGLISH SCONES

These citrus-studded scones transport you to English manors, flow-ered-scented rooms, starched linen, and the ritual of Devon cream and jam, even if you are sitting on a stool in the humblest of kitchens.

2   cups all-purpose flour
4   tablespoons granulated sugar
1½ teaspoons baking powder
½   teaspoon salt
4   tablespoons margarine, cut into tablespoons
2½ tablespoons candied lemon peel
¼   cup plus 3 to 4 tablespoons milk
    Additional milk, enough to brush tops of scones before and
    after baking

NOTES

❏ *Dough may be cut into wedges. Place wedges, 1 inch apart, on parchment-lined baking sheet.*
❏ *If scones brown during baking, it is not necessary to put them under the broiler. Brush tops with additional milk after baking.*
❏ *These scones will have a biscuit-like texture.*

1. Line baking sheet with parchment paper. Preheat oven to 425°F.

2. In a large bowl, sift together flour, sugar, baking powder, and salt. With an electric mixer set on low speed, beat margarine into flour mixture until margarine is evenly distributed and mixture resembles meal. Mix in lemon peel.

3. Add ¼ cup plus 3 tablespoons milk and beat until blended. Dough should be a bit crumbly, but should hold together. If necessary, add the remaining 1 tablespoon milk. Do not overmix.

4. Gather dough into a ball. Place dough on a lightly floured board and flatten slightly. Turn dough over and pat into a 6-inch circle, 1 inch thick. With a lightly floured 2½-inch round cutter, cut straight down through dough. To get 6 scones, rework dough scraps.

5. Place scones, 1 inch apart, on parchment-lined baking sheet. Brush tops of scones with additional milk.

6. Bake in the middle of oven for 15 minutes.

7. Remove from oven. Preheat broiler. Broil scones about 6 inches from heat for 1 minute, no longer. Remove from oven onto a wire rack and brush tops of scones with additional milk.

8. Serve hot with butter or clotted cream and strawberry preserves and a cup of coffee.

Cool remaining scones completely and cover.

YIELD: *6 scones*

29

BREADS

My preference is ripe Camembert spread on crusty bread dunked in café au lait.

—Jacques Pepin, author and television personality

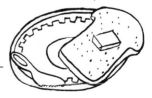

HONEY OAT BREAD

There is nothing as satisfying as a great piece of bread. Into your refrigerator overnight, out of your oven in the morning, this makes two delicately flavored loaves, perfect alone or for a delicious sandwich.

2   ¼-ounce packages active dry yeast
1   teaspoon granulated sugar
½   cup warm water, 110–115°F
1½ cups rolled oats, quick or regular
⅓   cup honey
4   tablespoons unsalted butter, cut into tablespoons
1   tablespoon salt
1   cup boiling water
1   cup sour cream
2   large eggs, lightly beaten
6½ cups sifted all-purpose flour, divided
    Additional all-purpose flour, enough to knead dough (¼ to ½ cup)
    Additional unsalted butter, enough to rub on top of baked bread (1 tablespoon)

1. Grease two 5½- by 9½-inch loaf pans.

2. Sprinkle yeast and sugar over the ½ cup warm water. Stir to dissolve and let stand a few minutes until foamy.

3. In a large bowl and with an electric mixer set on medium-low speed, beat together oats, honey, the 4 tablespoons butter, salt, and the 1 cup boiling water until butter is melted, 1 minute. Add sour cream and beat until mixture is lukewarm, 1 minute.

4. Reduce mixer speed to low. Add the dissolved yeast, eggs, and 2 cups of the 6½ cups flour and beat until smooth, 1 minute. Gradually add the remaining 4½ cups flour and continue to beat until all of the flour is incorporated. This will be a lot of dough; it will force its way up and around the upper part of the beater. Stop mixer and, with a rubber spatula, release dough from beater, pushing it back down into the bowl as necessary.

5. On a lightly floured wooden board, knead dough for 5 minutes, adding additional flour as needed to keep dough from sticking to board. Do not add any more flour than necessary and no more than ½ cup. Cover dough with clean dish towel and let rest for 20 minutes. Divide dough into two equal portions.

6. Place dough in prepared pans. Cover with plastic wrap and refrigerate several hours or overnight. The dough will rise slightly.

7. Preheat oven to 375°F. Let dough stand at room temperature for 10 minutes before baking.

8. Bake in the middle of oven for 40 minutes or until top is golden brown and bread sounds hollow when tapped.

9. Remove from oven and immediately turn out onto a wire rack so that the top of the bread is facing up. Rub with the 1 tablespoon butter and cool for at least 20 minutes.

10. Cut into slices. Serve warm or at room temperature with a cup of coffee.

Cool remaining bread completely and cover.

YIELD: *2 loaves*

BUTTERY CRESCENT ROLLS

Satisfaction is guaranteed with these tender, golden yeast rolls contributed by Rita Nader Heikenfeld, CCP, food columnist, cooking instructor, and radio and television personality based in Cincinnati, Ohio.

"My coffee thoughts," Rita confides, "center around my childhood and young adulthood before I left home. Coffee was always brewing on the stove and often it was the only drink my parents had to offer guests as they entered. (With a family of eleven, there wasn't extra in the budget.) My parents bought their coffee at the local grocer, whole beans, which they ground themselves. On special occasions, my dad would brew Lebanese (Greek) coffee in his ancient copper long-handled pot. I still have that pot, and it sits in my kitchen. Whenever I glance at it, warm coffee thoughts of my mother's kitchen envelop me."

NOTE

❏ *Skim milk may be substituted for whole milk. The ⅓ cup sugar may be reduced to ¼ cup. The rolls turn out great either way.*

8 tablespoons butter, cut into tablespoons
⅓ cup granulated sugar, divided
½ cup milk, scalded
1 ¼-ounce package active dry yeast, regular or rapid-rise
½ cup warm water, 110–115°F
1 large egg, lightly beaten
4 cups all-purpose flour, divided
4 tablespoons butter, very soft
4 tablespoons butter, melted

1. Place the 8 tablespoons butter and all but ⅛ teaspoon of the ⅓ cup sugar in a large bowl. Pour hot milk over butter and sugar and with an electric mixer set on low speed, beat until butter is melted. Cool to lukewarm.

2. Sprinkle yeast and the reserved ⅛ teaspoon sugar over warm water. Stir to dissolve and let stand a few minutes until foamy.

3. With the electric mixer set on low speed, beat dissolved yeast and egg into milk mixture.

4. Gradually add 2½ cups of the 4 cups flour and beat until smooth, 1 minute. Increase mixer speed to medium and beat until mixture is thick, 3 minutes. Reduce mixer speed to low and add the remaining 1½ cups flour, a little at a time, to make a dough that is medium-soft, but leaves the sides of the bowl.

5. On a lightly floured wooden board, knead dough until it can be gathered into a smooth ball, 1 minute.

34

6. In a large buttered bowl, turn dough until it is completely coated with butter. Cover and let rise in warm place until doubled, 1 hour to 1 hour and 30 minutes.

7. Line baking sheets with parchment paper.

8. Punch down dough. Turn out onto the lightly floured wooden board and divide into two equal portions. Cover and let rest for 10 minutes.

9. Roll one portion of dough into a 10- to 12-inch circle and spread with 2 tablespoons of the 4 tablespoons very soft butter. Cut dough into 12 wedges. Roll up each wedge beginning with wide end. Curve each wedge into a crescent or horn shape.

10. Place rolls, seam side down, on parchment-lined baking sheets. Cover and let rise until doubled, 30 to 45 minutes. Repeat with remaining portion.

11. Preheat oven to 375°F.

12. Bake in the middle of oven, one sheet at a time, for 15 to 20 minutes or until golden brown.

13. Remove from oven and immediately brush rolls with the melted butter.

14. Serve warm with your favorite savory or sweet spreadable and a cup of coffee.

Cool remaining rolls completely and cover.

YIELD: *24 rolls*

EPISCOPALIAN SODA BREAD

This beautiful-looking loaf combines textures and tastes with plump moist raisins and the punch of savory caraway seeds. It makes a lovely gift.

2	cups all-purpose flour
1/2	cup granulated sugar
3/4	teaspoon baking powder
1/2	teaspoon baking soda
1/4	teaspoon salt
4	tablespoons unsalted butter, melted and cooled
1	cup buttermilk
1	large egg, lightly beaten
2	teaspoons caraway seeds
1	cup raisins

1. Grease a 4- by 8-inch loaf pan. Preheat oven to 350°F.

2. In a medium bowl, sift together flour, sugar, baking powder, baking soda, and salt. Add melted butter, buttermilk, and egg and, with a sturdy wooden spoon, stir until dry ingredients are just moistened and no pockets of flour remain. Stir in caraway seeds and raisins.

3. Spread batter evenly into prepared pan.

4. Bake in the middle of oven for 50 minutes or until toothpick inserted in center comes out clean.

5. Remove from oven onto a wire rack and cool in pan for 10 minutes. Remove bread from pan onto wire rack and cool completely.

6. Cut into slices. Serve at room temperature with a cup of coffee.

Cover remaining bread.

YIELD: *1 loaf*

IRISH CATHOLIC SODA BREAD

Irish soda breads are unique to those who make and eat them. This handsome version is more cake-like than the traditional one made with caraway seeds. Barbara brought a warm-from-the-oven loaf to Linda's home the day they met. This bread is as good as their friendship.

3 cups sifted all-purpose flour
1 teaspoon baking soda
½ teaspoon baking powder
½ teaspoon salt
¼ teaspoon cream of tartar
8 tablespoons margarine
½ cup granulated sugar
1½ cups buttermilk
1½ cups raisins

1. Grease a 9-inch pie tin. Line bottom and sides with wax or parchment paper; grease paper. Preheat oven to 350°F.

2. Sift together sifted flour, baking soda, baking powder, salt, and cream of tartar. Set aside.

3. In a large bowl and with an electric mixer set on medium speed, cream together margarine and sugar until light and fluffy.

4. Reduce mixer speed to low. Add flour mixture alternately with buttermilk, beating well after each addition, beginning and ending with flour mixture. Stop mixer and scrape down bottom and sides of bowl as necessary. Mix in raisins.

5. Spread batter evenly into prepared pan.

6. Bake in the middle of oven for 1 hour to 1 hour and 10 minutes or until toothpick inserted in center comes out clean.

7. Remove from oven onto a wire rack and cool in pan for 10 minutes. Remove bread from pan.

8. Cut into wedges. Serve warm with a cup of coffee.

Cool remaining bread completely and wrap in a cotton dish towel. After one day, wrap remaining bread in plastic wrap.

YIELD: *1 loaf*

ORANGE BLACK PEPPER BREAD

A double dose of orange and the perk of pepper give this loaf surprise and sophistication. Painting the warm loaf with orange syrup guarantees a juicy slice.

BREAD

3	cups sifted all-purpose flour
¾	teaspoon baking soda
¾	teaspoon baking powder
½	teaspoon salt
2	teaspoons freshly ground black pepper
1	cup unsalted butter, cut into tablespoons
	Grated zest of 2 oranges
1¾	cups granulated sugar
3	large eggs
4	tablespoons fresh orange juice
1	cup buttermilk

ORANGE SYRUP

⅓	cup fresh orange juice
½	cup granulated sugar

1. Grease two 4- by 8-inch loaf pans. Line bottoms of pans with wax or parchment paper; grease paper. Dust lightly with flour. Preheat oven to 325°F.

2. Sift together sifted flour, baking soda, baking powder, and salt. Mix in pepper. Set aside.

3. In a large bowl and with an electric mixer set on medium-low speed, cream together butter and zest until smooth. Add sugar and cream until light and fluffy. Add eggs, one at a time, beating well after each addition. Stop mixer and scrape down bottom and sides of bowl as necessary.

4. Set mixer on low speed. Add flour mixture alternately with orange juice and buttermilk, beating well after each addition, beginning and ending with flour mixture. Stop mixer and scrape down bottom and sides of bowl as necessary.

5. Spread batter evenly into prepared pans.

6. Bake in the middle of oven for 1 hour or until toothpick inserted in center comes out clean.

7. Remove from oven onto a wire rack and cool in pans for 20 minutes.

8. *Prepare orange syrup:* In a small heavy saucepan, combine orange juice and sugar. Cook over low heat until sugar is dissolved. Remove from heat.

9. To catch drips, place wire rack over a piece of wax paper. Remove bread from pans onto wire rack. Stir syrup with pastry brush before applying syrup to bread. Brush all sides of bread with syrup and cool completely.

10. Cut into slices. Serve at room temperature with a cup of coffee.

Cover remaining bread.

YIELD: *2 loaves*

PERSIMMON BREAD

Dave Foegley, chef of Peter's Restaurant and Bar in Indianapolis, Indiana, contributed this unusual quick bread recipe utilizing the unique taste of persimmon.

1³/₄ cups sifted all-purpose flour
1   cup granulated sugar
1   teaspoon baking soda
³/₄ teaspoon salt
¹/₂ teaspoon ground mace
8   tablespoons unsalted butter, melted and cooled
2   large eggs, lightly beaten
¹/₃ cup brandy
1   cup persimmon pulp
1   cup pecans, coarsely chopped
¹/₂ cup golden raisins

1. Lightly grease bottom and sides of a 5¹/₂- by 9¹/₂-inch loaf pan. Line bottom with wax or parchment paper; grease paper. Dust lightly with flour. Preheat oven to 350°F.

2. In a large bowl, sift together sifted flour, sugar, baking soda, and salt. Mix in mace. Make a well in the dry ingredients and add in order, without beating, melted butter, eggs, brandy, persimmon pulp, pecans, and golden raisins. With a sturdy wooden spoon, stir batter until dry ingredients are just moistened and no pockets of flour remain.

3. Spread batter evenly into prepared pan. The pan will be about ³/₄ full.

4. Bake in the middle of oven for 55 to 60 minutes or until toothpick inserted in center comes out clean.

5. Remove from oven onto a wire rack and cool in pan for 20 minutes. Remove bread from pan onto wire rack and cool completely.

6. Cut into slices. Serve at room temperature with a cup of coffee.

Cover remaining bread.

YIELD: *1 loaf*

BROWNIES, BARS, AND CHEWY, GOOEY COOKIES

Now that you ask, I guess I am quite fussy about my coffee. The cup can be important too. Good coffee is diminished by paper or foam cups. I don't prefer fine china for coffee—probably because I have rarely had great coffee in a delicate china cup. I prefer a small or medium-sized mug—not a giant mug and not one that has too thick of a rim. A stoneware mug is nice, if the rim is well made. I think this is a matter of association for me—my Berkeley friends who have stoneware mugs happen to make great coffee. I like handpainted cups from France, Spain, Portugal, or Italy but I guess this is getting a little off the subject.

—Alice Medrich, author of *Cocolat: Extraordinary Chocolate Desserts*
and *Chocolate and the Art of Low-Fat Desserts*

ESPRESSO BROWNIES

Earn serious brownie points with these intense chocolate and coffee-flavored brownies developed by Dawn Bailey, pastry chef at Wolf Coffee Company in Santa Rosa, California.

"I have been in the bakery," Dawn reveals, "since 3:00 A.M., busy for several hours before the early morning baking is done. I go into the café about 7:00 A.M. when the first urn of French Roast has just finished brewing. We open the doors to welcome the first customers of the day with the aroma of freshly roasted and brewed coffee. I pour myself a cup—watching, listening, and sipping as the customers select one of my freshly baked scones, muffins, or brownies. It's a feeling of great satisfaction."

9 **ounces unsweetened chocolate, chopped**
1¼ cups unsalted butter, cut into tablespoons
¾ cup Wolf's roasted espresso beans, finely ground
3¼ cups granulated sugar
1¾ cups coarsely chopped walnuts
½ teaspoon salt
1½ teaspoons pure vanilla extract
6 large eggs
1¾ cups all-purpose flour

1. Line the bottom of a 9- by 13-inch baking pan with parchment paper; generously butter paper. Preheat oven to 300°F.

2. In a stainless steel bowl over gently simmering water, melt chocolate and butter, stirring until smooth. Remove from heat.

3. In a large bowl and with an electric mixer set on low speed, thoroughly mix together ground coffee and sugar. Increase mixer speed to medium. Gradually add melted chocolate mixture, walnuts, salt, and vanilla and beat until thoroughly combined. Add eggs one at a time, beating well after each addition.

4. Reduce mixer speed to low. Gradually add flour, beating until just incorporated.

5. Spread batter evenly into prepared pan.

6. Bake in the middle of oven for 55 to 60 minutes or until top is glossy and toothpick inserted in center comes out almost clean.

7. Remove from oven onto a wire rack and cool completely.

8. Cut into 3- by 2½-inch almost squares. Serve at room temperature with a cup of coffee.

Cover remaining brownies.

YIELD: *15 brownies*

FROSTED CITRUS MARMALADE SQUARES

Portion control is a problem with these gooey adult bar cookies. To put more goo in the gooey, slightly underbake.

NOTE

❑ *Leaving the border prevents the filling from sticking to sides of pan.*

FILLING

1   12-ounce jar (1 cup) orange marmalade
½   cup chopped pecans
½   cup sweetened, shredded coconut

COOKIE DOUGH

1½ cups sifted all-purpose flour
1   teaspoon baking powder
¼   teaspoon baking soda
¼   teaspoon salt
8   tablespoons unsalted butter, cut into tablespoons
1   cup firmly packed light brown sugar
2   tablespoons fresh orange juice (½ orange)
1   teaspoon pure vanilla extract
1   large egg
1   cup quick-cooking rolled oats

ORANGE FROSTING

1   cup sifted confectioners' sugar
½   tablespoon unsalted butter, room temperature
1   tablespoon fresh orange juice

1. Generously grease a 9-inch square baking pan. Preheat oven to 350°F.

2. *Prepare filling:* In a small bowl, combine marmalade, pecans, and coconut. Set aside.

3. Sift together sifted flour, baking powder, baking soda, and salt. Set aside.

4. In a large bowl and with an electric mixer set on medium speed, cream together butter and brown sugar until smooth. Beat in orange juice and vanilla until thoroughly combined. Add egg and beat.

5. Reduce mixer speed to low. Gradually add flour mixture, beating until just incorporated.

6. Stir in rolled oats by hand.

7. Spread half of the cookie dough evenly into prepared pan, forming a thin layer. Leaving a ½-inch border, gently smooth spoonfuls of filling over dough. Drop spoonfuls of remaining dough over filling and, with the back of a clean spoon or your fingertips, carefully spread to edges of pan. Take your time; it's worth the treat.

8. Bake in the middle of oven for 40 minutes or until top is golden brown.

9. Remove from oven onto a wire rack and cool completely.

10. *Prepare frosting:* In a medium bowl, whisk together sifted confectioners' sugar, butter, and orange juice until smooth.

11. Spread top evenly with frosting. Let frosting set for 20 minutes.

12. Cut into 1½-inch squares. Serve at room temperature with a cup of coffee.

Cover remaining squares.

YIELD: *36 squares*

LEMON BARS

Cathy Peachey Metzger, the late chef-proprietor, and Martha Voigt, pastry chef, of CATH, Inc., in Indianapolis, Indiana, developed this recipe for her popular coffee houses. The dreamy lemon filling covers a crust that truly melts in your mouth.

Norman Metzger, Cathy's husband, remembers, "CATH, Inc. (Coffee and Tea House) was much more than a business to Cath. It was an extension of her persona and her personality. Her status in the community was tied to this business and it gave her many opportunities to contribute to the community. More so than most businesses, coffee is a 'feel good' enterprise and Cath's love for her customers and people made for an ideal fit. Her customers loved to see her, talk to her, and just be with her in her stores. When they left, they always felt better."

NOTES

❑ *The crust may be made with an electric mixer set on low speed.*
❑ *The filling may be made in a food processor.*
❑ *We used fresh lemon juice. Bottled lemon juice must be shaken before using.*

CRUST

1   cup unsalted butter, cut into tablespoons
2   cups all-purpose flour
½   cup confectioners' sugar

LEMON FILLING

4   large eggs, lightly beaten
2   cups granulated sugar
½   teaspoon salt
4   tablespoons all-purpose flour
1   teaspoon baking powder
4   tablespoons lemon juice
    Confectioners' sugar, enough to dust finished bars

1. Butter a 9- by 13-inch baking pan. Line bottom of pan with parchment paper; butter paper. Preheat oven to 350°F.

2. *Prepare crust:* In a food processor, place butter, flour, and confectioners' sugar and pulse until mixture is crumbly. The mixture should resemble cornmeal, not pie dough. This blending happens quickly; do not overprocess.

3. Turn out crust mixture into prepared pan. Nudge mixture evenly into pan and pat firmly into place.

4. Bake in the middle of oven for 15 minutes or until edges are light brown.

5. Remove from oven onto a wire rack and cool for 15 minutes. Maintain oven temperature.

46

6. *Prepare filling:* In a large bowl and with an electric mixer set on medium-low speed, beat together eggs, sugar, and salt for 2 minutes. Gradually add flour, baking powder, and lemon juice and beat for an additional 2 minutes.

7. Pour filling evenly over crust and smooth top. Run a knife through the filling to remove air bubbles.

8. Bake in the middle of oven for 22 to 25 minutes or until top is lightly browned.

9. Remove from oven onto a wire rack and generously dust top of the bars with confectioners' sugar. Cool completely, 2 hours.

10. Cut into 3- by 2-inch bars. Serve at room temperature with a cup of coffee.

Cover remaining bars.

YIELD: *18 bars*

JOANNE'S BABY RUTH BARS

Fall absolutely in love with these chewy, chocolatey, peanutty, candy bar–like treats.

NOTES

❑ *If chocolate does not melt enough to spread over bars, place foil-covered pan in a 250°F oven just long enough to melt chocolate.*
❑ *If chocolate does not set at room temperature, refrigerate. Bars may be served chilled.*

½   **cup granulated sugar**
½   **cup firmly packed light brown sugar**
1   **cup light corn syrup**
1   **cup smooth peanut butter**
1   **cup salted Spanish peanuts**
6   **cups corn flakes**
4   **1.55-ounce milk chocolate candy bars, broken into pieces**

1. Set aside an ungreased 9- by 13-inch baking pan.

2. In a large heavy saucepan, combine granulated sugar, brown sugar, and corn syrup. Over medium-high heat, bring sugar mixture to a boil, stirring occasionally.

3. Remove from heat and add peanut butter, peanuts, and corn flakes. With a sturdy wooden spoon, stir until well mixed and corn flakes are thoroughly coated.

4. Immediately spread mixture evenly into ungreased pan. While warm, top with chocolate bar pieces. Cover pan with aluminum foil until chocolate melts, 10 minutes. Spread melted chocolate evenly over entire top like frosting.

5. Cut into 1½-inch squares. Cool in pan until chocolate is completely set; recut.

6. Serve at room temperature with a cup of coffee.

Store remaining bars in an airtight container.

YIELD: *45 bars*

JOE'S CHOCOLATE TOFFEE SCRUNCH COOKIES

This is the great all-around chocolate chipper. Joe has added extra toffee crunch.

2   cups all-purpose flour
1   teaspoon baking soda
½   teaspoon salt
8   tablespoons unsalted butter, room temperature, cut into tablespoons
½   cup solid shortening
¾   cup firmly packed light brown sugar
½   cup granulated sugar
1   large egg
2   teaspoons pure vanilla extract
1   12-ounce package (2 cups) semisweet chocolate chips
3   1.4-ounce milk chocolate butter toffee bars, preferably Hershey's Skor bars, coarsely chopped

1. Set aside ungreased baking sheets. Preheat oven to 375°F.

2. Sift together flour, baking soda, and salt. Set aside.

3. In a large bowl and with an electric mixer set on medium speed, cream together butter, shortening, brown sugar, and granulated sugar until smooth. Beat in egg and vanilla.

4. Reduce mixer speed to low. Gradually add flour mixture, beating until just incorporated. Stop mixer and scrape down bottom and sides of bowl as necessary.

5. Stir in chocolate chips and toffee pieces by hand.

6. Drop cookie dough by teaspoonfuls, 2 inches apart, onto ungreased cookie sheets.

7. Bake in the middle of oven, one sheet at a time, for 7 to 9 minutes. The cookies will appear somewhat underbaked, but will firm as they cool.

8. Remove from oven onto a wire rack. With a metal spatula, immediately scrunch edges toward center of each cookie, resulting in smaller, chunkier cookies. Cool on baking sheet for 5 minutes. With the metal spatula, transfer cookies onto wire rack and cool.

9. Serve warm or at room temperature with a cup of coffee.

Cool remaining cookies completely and store in an airtight container.

YIELD: *54 (2½-inch) cookies*   **49**

CHOCOLATE CHIP SPICE CROCODILES

This recipe is a gift from Marlene Sorosky, author of *Entertaining on the Run.* Such a good cookie, make it whenever and forever.

"Truthfully," Marlene confesses, "I never cared much for coffee. That is until several years ago when a friend mailed me a recipe for a favorite cookie. At the end of the recipe she wrote, 'And while they're still warm, sit down and enjoy with a good cup of coffee.' I laughed. Me, Miss Type A personality, sit down with a cup of coffee? I never even sat down for lunch. But while the cookies were baking, a small nagging voice inside repeated, 'Sit down and enjoy.' So I made a cup of coffee (not fresh brewed but the instant variety) and sat down. I remember thinking it was the best cookie I'd ever tasted. Since then whenever I want a special treat, I relax for a few minutes with a fresh home-baked cookie, like Chocolate Chip Spice Crocodiles, and a cup of hot coffee—still instant."

2   cups all-purpose flour
1   teaspoon baking soda
1/2 teaspoon salt, or to taste
1 1/2 teaspoons ground cinnamon
1 1/2 teaspoons ground ginger
1   cup butter or margarine, room temperature
1 1/3 cups firmly packed light brown sugar
1   large egg
1   teaspoon pure vanilla extract
1   12-ounce package (2 cups) semisweet chocolate chips
1   cup chopped walnuts
1   cup confectioners' sugar, for rolling cookies before baking

1. Sift together flour, baking soda, salt, cinnamon, and ginger. Set aside.

2. In a large bowl and with an electric mixer set on medium speed, cream together butter and brown sugar until smooth. Beat in egg and vanilla.

3. Reduce mixer speed to low. Add flour mixture, beating until just incorporated. Mix in chocolate chips and walnuts. Refrigerate dough until firm.

4. Pinch off pieces of dough and shape into 1-inch balls. Place balls on plates and refrigerate, covered with plastic wrap, for 2 to 3 hours or overnight.

5. Lightly grease baking sheets. Preheat oven to 350°F.

6. Place confectioners' sugar in a shallow bowl. Roll balls in sugar to coat thickly.

7. Place balls, 2 inches apart, on prepared baking sheets.

8. Bake in the upper third of oven, one sheet at a time, for 10 to 12 minutes or until tops look puffed, barely set, and cracked. The cookies will be very soft, but will firm as they cool. Do not overbake or they will be dry.

9. Remove from oven onto a wire rack and cool on baking sheet for 2 to 3 minutes. With a metal spatula, transfer cookies onto wire rack and cool.

10. Serve warm or at room temperature with a cup of coffee.

Cool remaining cookies completely and store in an airtight container.

YIELD: *72 cookies*

BISCOTTI, MANDEL BREAD, AND CRISP, CRUNCHY COOKIES

Great coffee arrived in New York by way of coffee bars in 1991. We saw an opportunity, and started supplying the industry with unique, bake-from-scratch, easy-to-handle American products from our tiny home kitchen in New York City. We still bake from scratch, but now we ship daily from Long Island to Philadelphia, thousands of cookies, cakes, brownies, lemon bars, and pistachio logs. Our 4,000-square-foot kitchen runs 24 hours a day, 7 days a week, to supply the growing gourmet coffee industry.

—Eli and Leslie Richman, Owners, Oven Arts, Inc.,
New York, New York

CHOCOLATE CHIP AND ALMOND BISCOTTI

New to biscotti? Make the transition with this original recipe from Lisa Ann Straub, pastry chef of The Beekman 1766 Tavern in Rhinebeck, New York.

Lisa says, "Reaction is everything. I love the excitement in people's faces when they try one of these great chocolate and almond cookies. Maybe this biscotti recipe is a little twist on the basic chocolate chip cookie . . . an Italian twist."

3¼ cups all-purpose flour
³/₄ teaspoon baking soda
³/₄ teaspoon baking powder
12 tablespoons unsalted butter, room temperature, cut into tablespoons
1³/₄ cups granulated sugar
1 teaspoon pure vanilla extract
3 large eggs
1¹/₂ cups sliced almonds
1 6-ounce package (1 cup) semisweet chocolate chips

1. Sift together flour, baking soda, and baking powder. Set aside.

2. In a large bowl and with an electric mixer set on medium speed, cream together butter, sugar, and vanilla until smooth. Add eggs, one at a time, beating well after each addition. Mix in almonds and chocolate chips.

3. Reduce mixer speed to low. Gradually add flour mixture, beating until just incorporated. Cover and refrigerate for at least 2 hours or overnight.

4. Line a baking sheet with parchment paper. Preheat oven to 350°F.

5. Divide cookie dough into two equal portions. Shape each portion into a 2- by 16-inch log.

6. Place logs, 3 inches apart, on parchment-lined baking sheet.

7. Bake in the middle of oven for 35 to 40 minutes.

8. Remove from oven onto a wire rack and cool on baking sheet. Lower oven temperature to 325°F.

9. With a sharp knife, slice logs diagonally into ¹/₂-inch widths. Place biscotti, flat side down, on ungreased, unlined baking sheets and bake until golden brown.

10. Remove from oven. With a metal spatula, transfer biscotti onto wire rack and cool completely.

11. Serve at room temperature with a cup of coffee.

Store remaining biscotti in an airtight container.

YIELD: *60 biscotti*

HAZELNUT BISCOTTI

Give in to temptation with these toasted hazelnut cookies created by John Ash, culinary director of the Fetzer Valley Oaks Food and Wine Center in Hopland, California.

"Rich, strong coffee has to be paired with something crisp and 'dunkable.' I think this Hazelnut Biscotti is a match made in heaven," John concludes.

3 cups all-purpose flour
2 teaspoons baking powder
¼ teaspoon salt
1 cup granulated sugar
8 tablespoons unsalted butter, melted and cooled
4 tablespoons hazelnut liqueur or brandy
1 cup hazelnuts, lightly toasted, skinned, and coarsely chopped
3 large eggs

1. Line a baking sheet with parchment paper. Preheat oven to 350°F.

2. Sift together flour, baking powder, and salt. Set aside.

3. In a large bowl and with an electric mixer set on medium speed, beat together sugar, melted butter, liqueur, hazelnuts, and eggs.

4. With a sturdy wooden spoon, stir in flour mixture.

5. With lightly floured hands, knead briefly. Divide cookie dough into two equal portions. Shape each portion into a long loaf about 2 inches in diameter.

6. Place loaves, 3 inches apart, on parchment-lined baking sheet.

7. Bake in the middle of oven for 25 minutes or until firm. It will have a cake-like texture.

8. Remove from oven onto a wire rack and cool on baking sheet for 10 minutes. Maintain oven temperature.

9. With a sharp knife, slice loaves diagonally into ½-inch widths. Place biscotti, flat side down, on ungreased, unlined baking sheets. Bake for an additional 20 minutes, turning them once, or until both sides are lightly browned and toasted.

10. Remove from oven. With a metal spatula, transfer biscotti onto wire rack and cool completely.

11. Serve at room temperature with a cup of coffee.

Store remaining biscotti in an airtight container.

56

YIELD: *40 biscotti*

WALNUT MANDEL BREAD

This biscotti-like walnut cookie is dredged in sugar and spice. If you leave them to crisp in the oven overnight, you can wake up to this delight.

1	cup granulated sugar
½	cup corn oil
2	large eggs
1½	teaspoons pure vanilla extract
2½	cups all-purpose flour
½	teaspoon baking powder
1	cup coarsely chopped walnuts
2	tablespoons granulated sugar
¼	teaspoon ground cinnamon

NOTE

❏ *This recipe may be doubled.*

1. Line baking sheet with parchment paper. Preheat oven to 350°F.

2. In a large bowl and with a sturdy wooden spoon, stir the 1 cup sugar, oil, eggs, and vanilla until well combined. Combine flour and baking powder and stir into batter until dry ingredients are just incorporated. Stir in walnuts.

3. With lightly floured hands, divide cookie dough into two equal portions. Shape each portion into a 2- by 10-inch log.

4. Place logs, 2 inches apart, on parchment-lined baking sheet.

5. Combine the 2 tablespoons sugar and cinnamon. Sprinkle logs with cinnamon sugar and pat lightly.

6. Bake in the middle of oven for 25 to 30 minutes or until golden brown.

7. Remove from oven onto a wire rack and cool on baking sheet for 10 minutes. Maintain oven temperature.

8. With a sharp knife, slice logs into ½-inch widths. Place cookies, flat side down, on ungreased, unlined baking sheets and bake for an additional 10 minutes. Turn off oven and leave mandel bread in oven to crisp several hours or overnight.

9. Serve at room temperature with a cup of coffee.

Store remaining mandel bread in an airtight container.

YIELD: *40 cookies*

MOM'S MANDEL BREAD

Bobbie Hinman, co-author of the *Lean and Luscious Cookbook* series and author of *The Meatless Gourmet: Favorite Recipes from Around the World*, shares this heirloom recipe and childhood memory.

"This is my mom's (Min Greenberg) recipe. When I was growing up, the cookie jar in our kitchen was always filled with Mom's Mandel Bread. One of my favorite memories as a child was being allowed to dunk the crunchy cookies in coffee. It was a special treat, even though my 'coffee' then consisted of a cup of warm milk with a little coffee mixed in. Now when I visit Mom, her cookie jar is still always full and I love the warm, nostalgic feelings of having a cup of 'real' coffee with her and, of course, enjoying her homemade mandel bread."

NOTES

❏ *These crescent-shaped cookies are similar to Italian biscotti.*
❏ *On special occasions, Mom adds chocolate chips, nuts, or raisins to these crunchy cookies. On very special occasions, she adds all three!*
❏ *We placed the loaves 2 inches apart on prepared baking sheet.*

8   tablespoons margarine, melted
½   cup granulated sugar
2   large eggs
1   teaspoon pure vanilla extract
1   teaspoon pure almond extract
2   cups all-purpose flour
1½ teaspoons baking powder
¼   teaspoon salt

1. Lightly oil a baking sheet. Preheat oven to 350°F.

2. In a large bowl and with an electric mixer set on medium speed, beat together melted margarine and sugar. Add eggs one at a time, beating well after each addition. Beat in extracts.

3. Sift together flour, baking powder, and salt. Add half of the flour mixture to first mixture and beat well. Stir in remaining flour mixture by hand, mixing well.

4. On prepared baking sheet, shape cookie dough into two loaves, each about 2 inches wide and 12 to 14 inches long.

5. Bake in the middle of oven for 25 minutes or until loaves are a light golden brown.

6. Remove from oven. Maintain oven temperature.

7. Cut logs crosswise into ¾-inch slices and turn slices on their side. Return baking sheet to oven. After 3 minutes, turn off oven and leave baking sheet in oven with the door closed until mandel bread is completely cooled.

8. Serve at room temperature with a cup of coffee.

Store remaining mandel bread in an airtight container.

YIELD: *36 cookies*

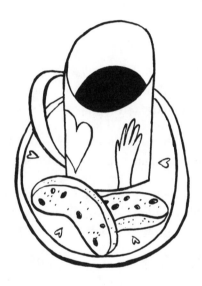

MARY'S FIVE-SPICE CHOCOLATE BISCOTTI

A great chocolate crunchy dunk. Mary and this dunk have spunk.

NOTE

❏ *A sharp knife is needed to cut cleanly through whole almonds.*

4   ounces semisweet chocolate, chopped
2   cups all-purpose flour
1/3   cup cocoa
1 1/2   teaspoons baking powder
1/4   teaspoon salt
1   tablespoon five-spice powder
3   large eggs
1/2   cup granulated sugar
1/2   cup firmly packed dark brown sugar
1   teaspoon pure almond extract
1 1/2   cups whole almonds, toasted in a 350°F oven for 7 to 10 minutes

1. In the top of a double boiler over gently simmering water, melt chocolate, stirring until smooth. Remove from heat.

2. Sift together flour, cocoa, baking powder, salt, and five-spice powder. Set aside.

3. In a large bowl and with an electric mixer set on medium speed, beat together eggs, granulated sugar, brown sugar, and almond extract.

4. Reduce mixer speed to low. Gradually add melted chocolate, beating until thoroughly blended. Stop mixer and scrape down bottom and sides of bowl as necessary. Gradually add flour mixture, beating until just incorporated. Mix in almonds.

5. Divide cookie dough into two equal portions. Dough will be sticky. On wax paper and with lightly floured hands, shape each portion into a 3- by 12-inch log. Wrap and refrigerate dough until firm.

6. Line baking sheet with parchment paper. Preheat oven to 300°F.

7. Place logs, 2 inches apart, on parchment-lined baking sheet.

8. Bake in the middle of oven for 40 minutes. Remove from oven onto a wire rack and cool on baking sheet for 10 minutes. Maintain oven temperature.

9. With a sharp knife, slice logs into 1/2-inch widths. Place bis-

cotti, flat side down, on ungreased, unlined baking sheets and bake for an additional 40 minutes.

10. Remove from oven. With a metal spatula, transfer biscotti onto wire rack and cool completely.

11. Serve at room temperature with a cup of coffee.

Store remaining biscotti in an airtight container.

YIELD: *48 biscotti*

SAFFRON BISCOTTI WITH APRICOTS AND PISTACHIOS

Gale Gand, chef-proprietor of Trio restaurant in Evanston, Illinois, presents this elegant cookie, richly spiced and gloriously colored.

"I was in New Zealand for a month," Gale recollects, "cooking with my husband at a restaurant in Auckland. We had been put up at a beautiful private hotel called Wiamanu, known for its exotic gardens and furnishings. So, wandering around the place, trying to take in all the beauty, I saw a forceful bush, at least ten feet tall, in the foyer, with stunning red berries salt-and-peppered on it. When I asked what sort it was, I learned it was . . . a coffee bush!"

½ teaspoon saffron threads, loose
2 tablespoons fresh orange juice
8 tablespoons unsalted butter, cut into tablespoons
1 cup granulated sugar
2 large eggs
¾ teaspoon pure vanilla extract
1½ teaspoons baking powder
¼ teaspoon salt
½ teaspoon plus ⅛ teaspoon ground cloves
2½ cups plus 2 tablespoons all-purpose flour
⅔ cup whole pistachios
¾ cup chopped dried apricots

1. Line a baking sheet with parchment paper. Preheat oven to 350°F.

2. In a small heavy saucepan over medium heat, warm together saffron and orange juice, stirring occasionally. Remove from heat.

3. In a large bowl and with an electric mixer set on medium speed, cream butter. Add sugar and whip until fluffy. Add eggs and vanilla, whipping until fluffy. Beat in warmed orange juice mixture.

4. Combine baking powder, salt, and cloves and beat into batter.

5. With a sturdy wooden spoon, stir in flour, pistachios, and apricots.

6. Divide cookie dough into two equal portions. With floured hands, shape each portion into a 13-inch log.

7. Place logs, 2 inches apart, on parchment-lined baking sheet.

8. Bake in the middle of oven for 20 to 25 minutes. Remove from oven onto a wire rack and cool on baking sheet for 5 minutes. Maintain oven temperature.

9. With a sharp knife, slice logs diagonally into ¼-inch widths. Place biscotti, flat side down, on ungreased, unlined baking sheets and toast for 10 minutes longer.

10. Remove from oven. With a metal spatula, transfer biscotti onto wire rack and cool completely.

11. Serve at room temperature with a cup of coffee.

Store remaining biscotti in an airtight container.

YIELD: *100 biscotti*

GREAT-GRANNY'S VANILLA CRISPS

This light and luscious melt-in-your-mouth cookie is destined to become a family heirloom. Good anytime, anywhere.

1 $^1/_2$ cups all-purpose flour
$^1/_2$ teaspoon baking soda
8   tablespoons butter, room temperature, cut into tablespoons
8   tablespoons margarine
$^3/_4$ cup granulated sugar
1   teaspoon distilled white vinegar
1   teaspoon pure vanilla extract
    Confectioners' sugar, enough to generously dust cookies

1. Set aside ungreased baking sheets. Preheat oven to 300°F.

2. Sift together flour and baking soda. Set aside.

3. In a large bowl and with an electric mixer set on medium speed, cream together butter, margarine, and sugar until smooth. Beat in vinegar and vanilla.

4. Reduce mixer speed to low. Gradually add flour mixture, beating until just incorporated.

5. Drop cookie dough by scant iced tea–spoonfuls, 2 inches apart, onto ungreased baking sheets.

6. Bake in the middle of oven, one sheet at a time, for 17 to 20 minutes or until golden.

7. Remove from oven onto a wire rack and cool on baking sheet for 5 minutes. With a metal spatula, transfer cookies onto wire rack and cool completely. Place wire rack over a piece of wax paper. Generously dust cookies with confectioners' sugar.

8. Serve at room temperature with a cup of coffee.

Store remaining cookies in an airtight container.

YIELD: *60 (2-inch) cookies*

MAPLE PECAN SUGAR COOKIES

Conjure up visions of New England with this recipe from Susan Goss, chef-proprietor of Zinfandel restaurant in Chicago, Illinois. This truly American cookie is worth the search for maple sugar.

2 cups all-purpose flour
2/3 cup pecans, toasted in a 350°F oven for 7 to 10 minutes, finely chopped
1/2 cup granulated sugar
1/4 cup maple sugar
12 tablespoons unsalted butter, cut into 1-inch cubes
1 large egg
1 teaspoon pure vanilla extract
40 pecan halves, not toasted

NOTE

❏ *Maple sugar can be ordered from Zinfandel, 59 West Grand Avenue, Chicago, Illinois, 60610; (312) 257–1818.*

1. In a food processor, place flour, chopped pecans, granulated sugar, and maple sugar and process with the steel blade until nuts are very finely chopped.

2. Add butter and process until coarse crumbs form. Add egg and vanilla; pulse until dough forms.

3. Shape cookie dough into a flat disk, wrap in plastic wrap, and refrigerate for at least 2 hours. At this point, dough may be refrigerated for up to 5 days.

4. Line baking sheets with parchment paper. Preheat oven to 350°F.

5. On a lightly floured wooden board, roll out dough to 1/4 inch thick. Cut dough with a 2-inch round cookie cutter.

6. Place cookies, 1 inch apart, on parchment-lined baking sheets. Press pecan half into center of each cookie.

7. Bake in the middle of oven, one sheet at a time, for 12 to 15 minutes or until cookies are slightly colored.

8. Remove from oven. With a metal spatula, transfer cookies onto a wire rack and cool completely.

9. Serve at room temperature with a cup of coffee.

Store remaining cookies in an airtight container.

YIELD: *40 cookies*

MOLASSES SNAPS

This old-fashioned ginger cookie has a grandmother's personality. Fill your kitchen with spicy scents and tomorrow's memories.

2   cups all-purpose flour
2   teaspoons baking soda
½   teaspoon salt
1   teaspoon ground ginger
1   teaspoon ground cinnamon
½   teaspoon ground cloves
¾   cup lard
1   cup granulated sugar
1   large egg, lightly beaten
¼   cup dark molasses
     Granulated sugar, enough to coat one side of unbaked cookies

1. Line baking sheets with parchment paper. Preheat oven to 350°F.

2. Sift together flour, baking soda, salt, ginger, cinnamon, and cloves. Set aside.

3. In a large bowl and with an electric mixer set on medium speed, cream together lard and sugar until smooth. Add egg and molasses and beat well. Stop mixer and scrape down bottom and sides of bowl as necessary.

4. Set mixer on low speed. Gradually add flour mixture, beating until just incorporated.

5. Pinch off pieces of cookie dough and shape into 1-inch balls. Dip one side of each ball in sugar; coat generously.

6. Place balls, sugared side up, 2 inches apart, on parchment-lined baking sheets. With the bottom of a glass dipped in sugar or the palm of your hand, gently flatten.

7. Bake in the middle of oven, one sheet at a time, for 7 to 8 minutes or until tops look cracked.

8. Remove from oven onto a wire rack and cool on baking sheet for 5 minutes. With a metal spatula, transfer cookies onto wire rack and cool completely.

9. Serve at room temperature with a cup of coffee.

Store remaining cookies in an airtight container.

YIELD: *60 (2¼-inch) cookies*

TRIPLE ALMOND CHINESE COOKIES

Triple fortune awaits. A china plate of these and a pot of coffee win friends. Entertain with almonds every which way.

2½ cups all-purpose flour
1½ teaspoons baking powder
½ teaspoon salt
1   cup solid shortening
1   cup granulated sugar
1   large egg
1½ teaspoons pure almond extract
½ cup ground almonds
36 whole blanched almonds
1   large egg yolk
1   tablespoon water

NOTES

❏ *If perfection is your goal, after pressing almond into cookie dough, smooth cracks along edges with your fingertips.*
❏ *Slivered almonds may be substituted for whole blanched almonds.*

1. Line baking sheets with parchment paper. Preheat oven to 350°F.

2. Sift together flour, baking powder, and salt. Set aside.

3. In a large bowl and with an electric mixer set on medium speed, cream together shortening and sugar until smooth. Add egg, almond extract, and ground almonds and beat well.

4. Reduce mixer speed to low. Gradually add flour mixture, beating until just incorporated.

5. Pinch off pieces of cookie dough and shape into 1-inch balls.

6. Place balls, 1½ inches apart, on parchment-lined baking sheets. Lightly press whole almond into center of each cookie.

7. Mix together egg yolk and water. Brush cookies with egg wash.

8. Bake in the middle of oven, one sheet at a time, for 17 to 20 minutes or until golden.

9. Remove from oven onto a wire rack and cool on baking sheet for 5 minutes. With a metal spatula, transfer cookies onto wire rack and cool completely.

10. Serve at room temperature with a cup of coffee.

Store remaining cookies in an airtight container.

YIELD: *36 cookies*

FANCY BITES, PASTRIES, AND CONFECTIONS

In Cajun Louisiana we have two kinds of coffee: **strong** *and* **weak**. **Weak** *coffee is very dark and rich. When you stir it with a spoon and let go of that spoon, it will stand straight up in the center of the cup.* **Strong** *coffee is also very dark, full of aroma and very rich. When you stir it with a spoon, the spoon* **dissolves**!

—Jude W. Theriot, CCP, traveling cooking teacher
and cookbook author

CHOCOLATE-DIPPED ALMOND HORSESHOE COOKIES

This almond-crusted, meringue-like cookie is a jewel and comes from the kitchen of The Kahler Plaza Hotel in Rochester, Minnesota.

NOTES

❑ *The egg whites should be at room temperature and free from contaminants and specks of egg yolk.*
❑ *For ease of rolling dough, use 2 cups crushed almonds. Some almonds will be left over; reserve for another use.*
❑ *If dough segment breaks apart when transferred to baking sheet, gently press dough together to re-form horseshoe shape.*

2   **cups (6 ounces) sliced almonds, lightly crushed**
7   **ounces almond paste, cut into 1-inch pieces**
1   **cup granulated sugar**
2   **large egg whites**
10   **ounces (1⅔ cups) bittersweet (not unsweetened) or semisweet chocolate, chopped**

1. Line baking sheets with parchment paper. Preheat oven to 375°F.

2. Spread out crushed almonds on a sheet of wax paper.

3. Place almond paste and sugar in a food processor; process until blended, 30 seconds. With machine running, gradually blend in egg whites. Turn off processor; scrape down sides of bowl. Continue processing for 20 seconds. Dough will be very sticky.

4. Spoon cookie dough into pastry bag fitted with a ½-inch plain round tip. Pipe a 3-inch-long segment of dough atop almonds. Gently roll dough in almonds, coating completely. Bend into horseshoe shape.

5. Carefully transfer horseshoe segment onto parchment-lined baking sheet, spacing cookies 1 inch apart. Repeat with remaining dough and almonds.

6. Bake in the middle of oven, one sheet at a time, for 15 minutes or until golden brown.

7. Remove from oven onto a wire rack and cool on baking sheet for 5 minutes. With a metal spatula, carefully transfer cookies onto wire rack and cool completely.

8. Meanwhile, in the top of a double boiler over gently simmering water, melt chocolate, stirring until smooth. Remove from heat.

9. Line a baking sheet with aluminum foil. Dip ends of cookie in melted chocolate, tilting pan as necessary. Shake cookie gently to remove excess chocolate. Place cookie, rounded side up, on foil-lined baking sheet. Repeat with remaining cookies. Refrigerate cookies until chocolate sets.

10. Fifteen minutes before serving, remove cookies from refrigerator. Serve at room temperature with a cup of coffee.

Store remaining cookies in an airtight container and refrigerate.

YIELD: *25 cookies*

CHOCOLATE NUT PUFFS

Whip up compliments. These addictive chocolate meringues are best served the day they are made. That should be no problem.

NOTES

❑ *The egg whites should be at room temperature and free from contaminants and specks of egg yolk.*
❑ *If melted chocolate becomes too cool, it is difficult to incorporate into egg white mixture.*

1   **6-ounce package (1 cup) semisweet chocolate chips**
2   **large egg whites, room temperature**
⅛   **teaspoon salt**
½   **cup granulated sugar**
½   **teaspoon distilled white vinegar**
½   **teaspoon pure vanilla extract**
¾   **cup chopped pecans, toasted in a 350°F oven for 6 to 8 minutes**

1. Line baking sheets with parchment paper. Preheat oven to 350°F.

2. In the top of a double boiler over gently simmering water, melt chocolate, stirring until smooth. Remove from heat.

3. In a clean, dry, large bowl, and with an electric mixer set on medium-low speed, beat egg whites and salt until foamy. Increase mixer speed to medium-high and gradually add sugar, beating continuously until the meringue is stiff and glossy, 5 to 6 minutes. Add vinegar and vanilla in last minute of whipping.

4. With a rubber spatula, fold in melted chocolate and pecans until chocolate is thoroughly incorporated.

5. Drop meringue by rounded teaspoonfuls, 1 inch apart, onto parchment-lined baking sheets.

6. Bake in the upper third of oven, one sheet at a time, for 10 minutes. The puffs will appear somewhat underbaked, but will firm as they cool.

7. Remove from oven onto a wire rack and cool on baking sheet for 10 minutes. With a metal spatula, transfer puffs onto wire rack and cool completely.

8. Serve at room temperature with a cup of coffee.

Store remaining puffs in an airtight container.

YIELD: *32 (2-inch) puffs*

ORANGE ALMOND FLORENTINES

Add flair to the occasion with this aristocratic cookie. Store in the freezer and present them at a moment's notice.

1	cup granulated sugar
2	large eggs
3	tablespoons sifted all-purpose flour
1/8	teaspoon baking powder
1/4	teaspoon salt
1/4	teaspoon ground cinnamon
1/8	teaspoon ground cloves
1/8	teaspoon grated nutmeg
1	cup finely chopped blanched almonds
1/4	cup chopped candied orange peel
1	teaspoon grated lemon zest (1/2 large lemon)

1. Line baking sheets with aluminum foil. Preheat oven to 400°F.

2. In a large bowl and with an electric mixer set on medium speed, beat sugar and eggs until light and lemon-colored, 2 to 3 minutes.

3. Reduce mixer speed to low. Gradually add sifted flour, baking powder, salt, cinnamon, cloves, and nutmeg, beating until just incorporated. Stop mixer and scrape down bottom and sides of bowl as necessary.

4. Stir in almonds, orange peel, and lemon zest by hand.

5. Drop cookie dough by teaspoonfuls, 3 inches apart, onto foil-lined baking sheets.

6. Bake in the middle of oven, one sheet at a time, for 6 to 7 minutes. The cookies will look very brown when done.

7. Remove from oven onto a wire rack and cool on baking sheet for 7 minutes. Carefully turn foil and cookies upside down. Peel foil from cookies the way you peel the backing off a name tag.

8. When cookies are completely cool, store them in layers, separated by wax paper, in an airtight container and freeze.

9. Moments before serving, remove cookies from freezer. Serve with a cup of coffee.

YIELD: *78 (2½-inch) cookies*

NOTES

❑ *It is important to pay close attention to the timing of this cookie, both the 6 to 7 minutes for baking and the 7 minutes for cooling.*

❑ *To retain crispness, cookies must be stored in the freezer.*

❑ *Chocolate lovers may spread a little melted chocolate over cookies.*

POPPY SEED SHORTBREAD

Here's a surprise: poppy seeds in shortbread! This is a delightful bite from Gale Gand, chef-proprietor of Trio restaurant in Evanston, Illinois.

1½ **cups unsalted butter, cut into tablespoons**
¾ **cup plus 2 tablespoons granulated sugar**
2¾ **cups all-purpose flour**
¾ **cup plus 2 tablespoons cornstarch**
¼ **cup poppy seeds**
2 **tablespoons granulated sugar, divided**

1. Line the bottom of a 10½- by 15½-inch sheet pan with parchment paper. Preheat oven to 350°F.

2. In a large bowl and with an electric mixer set on medium speed, cream together butter and the ¾ cup plus 2 tablespoons sugar until light and fluffy.

3. Reduce mixer speed to low. Add flour, cornstarch, and poppy seeds and blend until dough just comes together.

4. Pat cookie dough evenly into parchment-lined pan. With a rolling pin, roll dough to form an even layer. With a fork, pierce entire surface of dough. This helps air to escape during baking. Sprinkle dough with 1 tablespoon of the 2 tablespoons sugar.

5. Bake in the middle of oven for 20 to 30 minutes or until lightly colored. Rotate pan halfway through baking.

6. Remove from oven onto a wire rack and sprinkle top of the shortbread with the remaining 1 tablespoon sugar. Immediately cut into 2- by 1½-inch bars. Cool completely in pan.

7. Serve at room temperature with a cup of coffee.

Store remaining shortbread in an airtight container.

YIELD: *50 bars*

HAZELNUT TRUFFLES

Steven Keneipp, CCP, chef-proprietor of The Classic Kitchen in Noblesville, Indiana, shares his signature candy recipe.

Steve divulges, "I love the geography of coffee. When I drink Santos, I think of my favorite haunts in Brazil. When I drink Kona, I think of my time in the navy in Hawaii. When I drink Café Britt, I think of my second home, Costa Rica. It's a conjuring brew."

2	**cups whole hazelnuts**
7	**tablespoons unsalted butter**
1⅔	**cups heavy or whipping cream**
1	**pound Callebaut or Valrhôna bittersweet chocolate, finely chopped**
1	**tablespoon Frangelico or other hazelnut-flavored liqueur**

NOTE

❏ *Truffle mixture is firm when spoon stands straight up in the bowl. Mixture may be refrigerated several hours or overnight before rolling.*

1. Place hazelnuts in single layer on baking sheet and roast in a 350°F oven for 10 minutes or until fragrant. Place hot hazelnuts in heavy kitchen towel and rub off (and discard) loose skins. Let cool and chop very fine.

2. In a 3-quart heavy saucepan over medium heat, melt butter. Add cream and heat to boiling. Remove from heat and add chocolate and Frangelico. Whisk until chocolate is melted and mixture is smooth.

3. Turn mixture into a large bowl and refrigerate, stirring every half hour, until mixture firms evenly.

4. When firm, scoop chocolate mixture by rounded teaspoonfuls and roll in chopped nuts.

5. Cover and refrigerate in single layer until ready to serve.

6. Serve with a rich cup of coffee.

YIELD: *40 (1¼-inch) truffles*

FINGER FRETS

A neat little sour cream pastry that is perfect to pop in the oven and then in your mouth, and then in your mouth, and then in your mouth. Fret away the day.

NOTE

❏ *Dough may be refrigerated for up to 2 weeks. Make up each portion of dough as needed.*

3   **cups sifted all-purpose flour**
1   **¼-ounce package active dry yeast**
1   **cup butter, room temperature, cut into tablespoons**
1   **cup sour cream**
3   **large egg yolks**
1   **cup finely chopped pecans**
1   **cup granulated sugar**
1½ **teaspoons ground cinnamon**

1. In a large bowl, combine sifted flour and yeast. With clean fingertips or a wire pastry blender, cut in butter until flour mixture resembles coarse crumbs.

2. Mix together sour cream and egg yolks and add to flour mixture. With a sturdy wooden spoon, stir until well combined. Dough will be sticky.

3. Divide dough into four equal portions, wrap each portion in plastic wrap, and refrigerate for at least 4 hours or overnight.

4. Line baking sheets with parchment paper. Preheat oven to 325°F.

5. Combine pecans, sugar, and cinnamon. Scatter a fourth of the pecan mixture on a wooden board.

6. Shape one portion of the dough into a disk and coat both sides with the nut mixture. Roll out into a circle, ¼ inch thick, on top of nut mixture. Turn circle over and continue rolling until circle measures ¹⁄₁₆ inch thick, 11 inches in diameter. Cut circle into 16 wedges and roll each wedge, beginning with the rounded edge, into a fret.

7. Place each fret, with the pointed end on top, 1 inch apart, on parchment-lined baking sheet. Tuck or crimp point of fret to secure. Do not fret.

8. Bake in the middle of oven for 20 to 25 minutes or until golden. Do not overbake.

9. While frets are baking, repeat steps with another portion of dough.

10. Remove from oven onto a wire rack and cool on baking sheet for 5 minutes.

11. Serve warm or at room temperature with a cup of coffee.

Cool remaining frets completely and store in an airtight container.

YIELD: *64 frets*

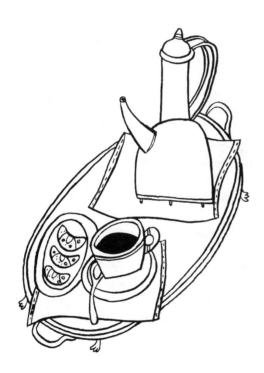

MINI-STRUDELS

Simply be prepared with this make-ahead, rich, sour cream dough. Then, laden it with thick apricot preserves, pecans, and coconut. This recipe was developed by Marcia Adams, author of *Cooking from Quilt Country; Heartland; Christmas in the Heartland;* and *Marcia Adams' Heirloom Recipes.* Marcia is also the host of *Marcia Adams' Kitchen* PBS series.

"One of my favorite ways to entertain friends," Marcia discloses, "is to invite them for afternoon coffee and then pass a tray of assorted pastries. And then we all just talk and talk and find out what everyone has done, and will be doing, including what books everyone is reading. I like to serve steaming hot coffee served in my grandmother's Haviland cups; it is the perfect foil for these delectable mini-strudels."

NOTES

❑ *Prepare the delicate butter-and-sour-cream pastry the day before rolling out the strudel.*
❑ *This pastry will not rise during baking, so you can bake all four rolls at the same time.*

1   cup butter (no substitutes)
1   cup sour cream
½   teaspoon salt
2½   cups all-purpose flour
2   12-ounce jars apricot preserves
2   cups chopped pecans
1   7-ounce container (generous 2 cups) shredded or flaked coconut
     Confectioners' sugar, enough to dust top of strudels

1. In a large saucepan over low heat, melt butter. Remove from heat and cool. Whisk in sour cream and salt. With a sturdy wooden spoon, stir in flour until well combined.

2. Divide pastry into four equal portions, wrap in plastic wrap, and refrigerate overnight.

3. Fifteen minutes before rolling out dough, remove pastry from refrigerator.

4. Set aside a 9- by 14-inch parchment-lined baking sheet. Preheat oven to 350°F.

5. On a lightly floured surface, roll out one portion of the dough into a 13- by 8-inch rectangle. The pastry should be very thin. Refrigerate remaining portions if pastry gets too soft at room temperature.

6. With a small rubber spatula, spread the pastry with half a jar of preserves, leaving one long side free of jam, about ¾ inch. Sprinkle on ½ cup pecans, and about ½ cup of the coconut. Roll up firmly, starting with the long jam-spread side. Crimp ends.

7. Transfer, seam side down, onto parchment-lined baking sheet. With a bread knife, cut through the top of the unbaked pastry at ½-inch intervals, cleaning knife as necessary. Do not cut all the way through the pastry.

8. Repeat with remaining portions, keeping filled pastries in refrigerator.

9. Bake in the middle of oven for 35 to 40 minutes.

10. Remove from oven onto a wire rack. With a metal spatula, immediately loosen rolls and allow the strudel to stand on baking sheet for 10 minutes. With the bread knife, finish cutting through the slices. Sift a bit of confectioners' sugar over top of the strudels and cool completely.

11. Serve at room temperature with a cup of coffee.

Store remaining pieces in layers, separated by wax paper, and freeze until needed.

YIELD: *75 pieces*

PRALINES EUPHEMIE

Satisfy your sweet tooth with this Cajun confection offered by Jude W. Theriot, CCP, traveling cooking teacher and author of *La Meilleure de la Louisiane* and *Cajun Healthy*.

"Coffee is an essential part of the life of a Louisiana Cajun. Even today," Jude allows, "I will drink five to ten cups a day. Anytime we gather, coffee is the glue that binds us and settles us down to serious work or not-so-serious play. When I go home (about four or five times a week), the first thing Momma does is put on a fresh pot of coffee. Coffee is made for sweets. It enhances and enlivens the 'sweet tooth.'

"I recall as a small boy (five or six years old) getting to drink *café au lait* (coffee milk) at my grandmother's house. She always made her grandsons feel special and important. We'd sneak into the kitchen with her and she'd fix us 'our coffee,' then she'd open a tin of wonderful pralines (which we pronounce 'praw leens'). The sweetness of the candy and the bitterness of the strong coffee, even though it was loaded with milk, still brings back so many wonderful memories and feelings. Euphemie Verret Borel was Grandma's name. This recipe is hers and like my memories of her it is special as she was special. A cup of coffee and Pralines Euphemie, that's my idea of 'the sum and substance of life and living.'"

NOTES

❏ *If candy mixture becomes too thick, stir in water, a little at a time, until mixture has desired consistency.*
❏ *We dropped candy mixture by the tablespoonful, yielding 80 smaller pralines.*

4	cups granulated sugar
2/3	cup firmly packed light brown sugar
1	cup evaporated milk
1/2	cup water
1/2	teaspoon salt
1/8	teaspoon ground cinnamon
2	cups whole pecans
2	cups pecan pieces
8	tablespoons unsalted butter
2	teaspoons pure vanilla extract

1. Line baking sheets with wax paper.

2. In a heavy, medium saucepan, mix together granulated sugar, brown sugar, evaporated milk, water, salt, and cinnamon. Over medium heat, bring the sugar mixture to a boil.

3. When sugar mixture comes to a boil, reduce heat to low and cook, stirring constantly, until a soft ball forms when a small amount

of mixture is dropped into cold water. Add pecans and cook, stirring, for 4 more minutes.

4. Remove from heat and add butter and vanilla. With a clean sturdy wooden spoon, beat until butter is completely melted and the candy mixture is creamy and all one color in appearance, about 1 or 2 minutes.

5. Drop candy mixture, 2 tablespoonfuls at a time, onto prepared baking sheets. Let pralines harden by standing at room temperature. Store pralines in a tightly covered container in a cool place for up to 1 week.

6. Serve at room temperature with a cup of coffee.

YIELD: *40 pralines*

COZY CAKES AND PUDDINGS

When we just opened the restaurant, it was in the late spring, going into summer. Days were very long and very hot. It became a ritual between my sous chef and myself that we would make for each other and drink several pitchers of iced coffee a day. Some days were fueled completely by that cold caffeine buzz. Now, whenever I see or drink iced coffee, I cannot help but remember those first days of the restaurant and the role those pitchers of iced coffee played in forming friendships, creating memories, and getting us through the day.

—Scott Peacock, Chef of Horseradish Grill in
Atlanta, Georgia, and co-founder of The Society for the Revival
and Preservation of Southern Food

PRUNE PUDDING CAKE WITH BUTTERMILK GLAZE

This rich, moist, sugar-and-spice cake is old-fashioned holiday goodness. Dessert or coffee cake, we can't decide.

NOTES

❑ *You may stew your own prunes or use canned cooked prunes. Drain prunes before measuring.*
❑ *If not using glaze immediately, beat until smooth before using.*
❑ *This cake may be served chilled.*

CAKE

2	**cups all-purpose flour**
1½	**cups granulated sugar**
1¼	**teaspoons baking soda**
1	**teaspoon baking powder**
½	**teaspoon salt**
1	**teaspoon ground nutmeg**
1	**teaspoon ground allspice**
1	**teaspoon ground cinnamon**
¾	**cup vegetable oil**
3	**large eggs, lightly beaten**
1	**cup buttermilk**
1	**teaspoon pure vanilla extract**
1	**cup cooked pitted prunes, chopped**
1	**cup chopped walnuts**

BUTTERMILK GLAZE

1	**cup granulated sugar**
4	**tablespoons unsalted butter, cut into tablespoons**
½	**teaspoon baking soda**
½	**cup buttermilk**
¼	**cup light corn syrup**
½	**teaspoon pure vanilla extract**

1. Grease and lightly flour a 9- by 13-inch baking pan. Preheat oven to 325°F.

2. In a large bowl, sift together flour, sugar, baking soda, baking powder, salt, nutmeg, allspice, and cinnamon. Make a well in dry ingredients and add in order, without mixing, oil, eggs, buttermilk, vanilla, prunes, and walnuts. With a sturdy wooden spoon, stir until thoroughly combined.

3. Pour batter evenly into prepared pan.

4. Bake in the middle of oven for 35 to 40 minutes or until cake pulls away from sides of pan, top is browned, and toothpick inserted in center comes out clean.

5. Ten minutes before cake is finished baking, *prepare Butter-*

milk Glaze: In a heavy medium saucepan, combine sugar, butter, baking soda, buttermilk, and corn syrup. Over medium heat, bring to a boil, stirring continuously. Boil, stirring, until glaze is a light caramel color, 10 minutes. Remove from heat and stir in vanilla.

6. Remove cake from oven onto a wire rack and immediately pour glaze over top of cake. Carefully tip cake pan to distribute glaze evenly and cool for at least 20 minutes.

7. Cut into squares. Serve warm or at room temperature with a cup of coffee.

Cool remaining cake completely, cover, and refrigerate.

YIELD: *15 servings*

NEW ORLEANS STYLE BREAD PUDDING WITH WHISKEY SAUCE

Try this new-fangled, old-fashioned bread pudding taught at The New Orleans School of Cooking in New Orleans, Louisiana.

"In my opinion," Larry Dauterive, general manager of the cooking school, offers, "nothing can beat a cup of *café au lait* at a New Orleans French Quarter coffee stand. The aroma of coffee with chicory is a wonderful way to start the day."

3	large eggs
2	cups granulated sugar
2	tablespoons pure vanilla extract
1	teaspoon ground cinnamon
$\frac{1}{2}$	teaspoon grated nutmeg
2	cups milk
2	cups heavy or whipping cream
	Day-old French bread, cut into $\frac{1}{2}$-inch cubes to equal 6 cups (20 slices, $\frac{1}{2}$ inch thick, about 8 ounces)
1	cup raisins
1	cup sweetened, shredded coconut
1	cup chopped pecans, toasted in a 350°F oven for 7 to 10 minutes
8	tablespoons unsalted butter, melted
	Whiskey Sauce (recipe follows)

1. Lightly butter a $2\frac{1}{2}$-quart shallow baking dish.

2. In a large bowl and with an electric mixer set on medium speed, beat together eggs, sugar, vanilla, cinnamon, and nutmeg. Reduce mixer speed to low and add milk and cream; continue beating until well mixed.

3. Place bread cubes in a separate large bowl. With a fine-mesh sieve, strain custard mixture over bread. Add raisins, coconut, and pecans and, with a sturdy wooden spoon or rubber spatula, toss to combine. Stir in melted butter. Let stand for 15 minutes so that the bread absorbs the liquid.

4. Preheat oven to 325°F.

5. Pour pudding mixture into prepared dish, distributing raisins, coconut, and pecans evenly.

6. Bake in the middle of oven for 1 hour and 10 minutes to 1 hour and 15 minutes or until custard is set (knife inserted 1 inch from center comes out clean) and top is golden brown. Cover pudding loosely with aluminum foil if pudding browns too quickly.

7. Remove from oven onto a wire rack and cool for at least 10 minutes.

8. Spoon onto serving plates. Serve warm with Whiskey Sauce (recipe follows), scant 2 tablespoons sauce for each serving, and a cup of coffee.

Cool remaining pudding completely, cover, and refrigerate.

YIELD: *9 servings*

WHISKEY SAUCE

8 tablespoons unsalted butter, cut into tablespoons
1½ cups confectioners' sugar, sifted
1 large egg yolk, lightly beaten
⅓ cup bourbon, or to taste

1. Place butter and sifted confectioners' sugar in a heavy medium saucepan. With a hand-held electric mixer set on low speed, cream together butter and sugar over medium heat until butter is absorbed. It will look like paste.

2. Remove from heat and beat in egg yolk. Gradually stir in bourbon. Sauce will thicken as it cools.

3. Serve warm.

Cool remaining sauce completely and refrigerate.

YIELD: *1 cup*

CANDIED CRANBERRY CAKE

This cake has everything—great taste, good looks, and ease of preparation. Fall in love with its satiny upper crust and caramelized cranberry crunch.

2   **cups fresh whole cranberries**
½   **cup chopped walnuts**
½   **cup granulated sugar**
2   **large eggs, lightly beaten**
1   **cup granulated sugar**
1   **cup all-purpose flour**
½   **teaspoon pure almond extract**
12   **tablespoons unsalted butter, melted and cooled**

1. Butter a 9-inch pie pan. Line bottom of pan with parchment paper; butter paper. Preheat oven to 350°F.

2. In a medium bowl, mix together cranberries, walnuts, and the ½ cup sugar. Spoon into prepared pan and distribute evenly.

3. In the same medium bowl, add, in order, eggs, the 1 cup sugar, flour, almond extract, and melted butter. With a sturdy wooden spoon, stir until smooth.

4. Pour batter evenly over cranberry mixture.

5. Bake in the middle of oven for 40 minutes or until toothpick inserted in center comes out clean.

6. Remove from oven onto a wire rack and cool for at least 30 minutes.

7. Cut into wedges. Serve warm or at room temperature with a cup of coffee.

Cool remaining cake completely and cover.

YIELD: *6 servings*

CHEWY DATE AND WALNUT CAKE

Any day is a holiday with this favored combination. Make this very quick fix for any sweet tooth.

1   **8-ounce box (1½ cups) pitted dates, coarsely chopped**
1½ **cups coarsely chopped walnuts**
1½ **cups confectioners' sugar**
2   **tablespoons all-purpose flour**
3   **large eggs, well beaten**

1. Grease and lightly flour an 8-inch round cake pan. Preheat oven to 325°F.

2. In a large bowl, mix together dates, walnuts, confectioners' sugar, and flour. Add beaten eggs and, with a sturdy wooden spoon, stir until well combined.

3. Spread batter evenly into prepared pan.

4. Bake in the middle of oven for 35 to 40 minutes or until top is golden and firm to the touch.

5. Remove from oven onto a wire rack and cool for at least 10 minutes.

6. Cut into wedges. Serve warm with a cup of coffee.

Cool remaining cake completely and cover.

YIELD: *6 servings*

NOTES

❑ *Use whole pitted dates and chop them, instead of using commercially chopped pitted dates.*

❑ *This dense cake may be topped with sweetened whipped cream.*

COZY COCONUT COOKIE CAKE

Doesn't it just sound delicious?

NOTES

❑ *An 11-ounce box of vanilla wafers gives you more than enough crumbs.*
❑ *This cake is plain good and good plain. If you feel compelled, garnish it with confectioners' sugar, fresh berries, or sweetened whipped cream.*

1	cup unsalted butter, room temperature
2	cups granulated sugar
6	large eggs
1	tablespoon pure vanilla extract
3	cups lightly packed vanilla wafer cookie crumbs
½	cup milk
1	7-ounce package (2⅔ cups lightly packed) sweetened, shredded coconut
1	cup chopped pecans, toasted in a 350°F oven for 7 to 10 minutes

1. Grease bottom and sides of a 10-inch tube pan. Line bottom of pan with wax or parchment paper; grease paper. Dust lightly with flour. Preheat oven to 300°F.

2. In a large bowl and with an electric mixer set on medium speed, cream butter until smooth. Add sugar, creaming until light and fluffy. Add eggs, one at a time, beating well after each addition. Stop mixer and scrape down bottom and sides of bowl as necessary. Beat in vanilla.

3. Reduce mixer speed to low. Add cookie crumbs alternately with milk, beating after each addition until smooth, beginning and ending with crumbs. Mix in coconut and pecans.

4. Spread batter evenly into prepared pan.

5. Bake in the middle of oven for 1 hour and 45 minutes to 1 hour and 50 minutes or until cake tester inserted in center comes out clean.

6. Remove from oven onto a wire rack and cool completely in pan, 2 hours.

7. To remove from pan, run a sharp knife along outside and inside edges of cake. Carefully invert onto a serving plate.

8. Cut into slices. Serve at room temperature with a cup of coffee.

Cover remaining cake.

YIELD: *12 servings*

PIES, TARTS, AND COBBLERS

I was raised in an enclave of coffee-drinking Scandinavians and Germans, whose dependence on other stimulants was limited to thimble-size drams of schnapps on important family occasions, but whose daily kaffeeklatsches were so indispensable that they drank the bracing liquid from china cups the size of tankards.

—Bert Greene,
the late food writer and television personality

PERFECT PIE PASTRY

This is the best. This recipe made Linda and Barbara successful pie makers at last. Join the legions of pie bakers that have come before us. Your mothers and grandmothers will be proud.

NOTES

❑ *Wooden board prevents pastry cloth from slipping.*
❑ *To freeze pie shells, place in plastic freezer bags. When ready to use, bake directly from freezer. For prebaked shells, prick before freezing.*

4½ cups sifted all-purpose flour
2 teaspoons salt
1½ cups solid shortening, cut into chunks
10 tablespoons ice water

1. In a large bowl, sift together sifted flour and salt. With a wire pastry blender, cut shortening into flour mixture until shortening is completely coated with flour and mixture resembles coarse crumbs. Use wires to pull up and lift flour mixture from bottom of bowl.

2. Remove ⅔ cup of flour mixture to a small bowl. Add ice water and, with a fork, mix until blended.

3. Add liquid mixture slowly to remaining flour mixture. With the fork, lift and toss until liquid mixture is absorbed and pastry dough comes away from sides of bowl and holds together. For ease of handling, chill dough for 30 minutes.

4. Place a pastry cloth on a large wooden cutting board. Lightly flour pastry cloth.

5. Form a smooth-sided disk with a fourth of the dough. Cover and refrigerate remaining dough until ready to roll out. Place disk on pastry cloth. With a sleeved rolling pin, roll dough from center upward, then from center downward. Turn 90 degrees and repeat.

6. Flip dough over. Reshape disk, smoothing edges. Starting from center of dough, begin rolling dough into a circle. Make sure dough is an even ⅛ inch thick.

7. Fold dough to form a half circle. Bring corners of straight edge to center of curved edge. Carefully place dough wedge into pie pan and unfold. With your fingertips, start from sides of pie shell and ease dough into pan, gently pressing dough smoothly into crease and sides.

8. To make crimped edge, trim dough evenly about ½ inch larger than pie pan. Form a wall at top of pie pan by folding under overlapping dough, pressing dough lightly together before crimping. (For double-crust pie, see Berry Cherry Pie, page 94.) For single-crust pie, proceed with step 9.

9. Crimp. Lightly flour your fingertips. Use thumb and index fin-

ger of your left hand to form a V on the inside edge of dough wall. Use index finger of your right hand to press rather strongly on outside edge into V. Continue around wall. Crimps should be close together.

10. Store pie shell in refrigerator while preparing filling, or cover and freeze.

11. For prebaked pie shells, preheat oven to 425°F. With the tines of a fork, prick sides and bottom of dough. Bake in the lower third of oven for 8 minutes. Lower oven temperature to 350°F and bake until crust is golden brown, 4 minutes. Remove from oven onto a wire rack.

12. Repeat steps with remainder of dough.

YIELD: *4 (9-inch) single crusts*

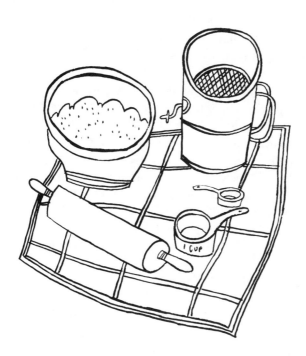

BERRY CHERRY PIE

A super-delicious blend of summer fruits in our Perfect Pie Pastry. Everyone will want this recipe. Go ahead and share.

Pastry for an 8-inch double-crust pie (Perfect Pie Pastry, page 92, ½ recipe)
- ¼   **cup all-purpose flour**
- 1   **cup granulated sugar**
- ½   **teaspoon ground cinnamon**
- 1   **cup fresh raspberries**
- 1   **cup fresh blueberries**
- 1   **cup drained canned tart red water-packed cherries**
- 2   **tablespoons unsalted butter, cut into small pieces**
     Confectioners' sugar, enough to dust top of pie

1. Preheat oven to 400°F. To catch drips, place baking sheet or a piece of aluminum foil on lower oven rack.

2. Prepare ½ recipe of Perfect Pie Pastry (page 92), steps 1 through 8. Do not crimp.

3. In a large bowl, combine flour, sugar, and cinnamon. Add berries and cherries and, with a rubber spatula, toss gently to coat fruit.

4. Fill pie shell with fruit mixture and dot with butter.

5. Roll out remaining pastry dough into a 10-inch circle. Carefully fold circle in half, center pastry over filling, and unfold. Trim top crust to extend ½ inch beyond bottom crust. Dampen outer wall of bottom crust with a bit of cold water. With lightly floured fingertips, form seal by pressing edge of top crust over outside edge of wall of bottom crust. Crimp the wall as described in step 9 of Perfect Pie Pastry (page 92). Cut several slits in top crust to allow steam to escape.

6. Bake in the middle of oven for 45 to 50 minutes or until crust is lightly browned and filling begins to bubble up through slits. Cover edge of crust loosely with aluminum foil if edge browns too quickly.

7. Remove from oven onto a wire rack and cool completely. Dust pie with confectioners' sugar.

8. Cut into wedges. Serve at room temperature with a cup of coffee.

Cover remaining pie.

94   **YIELD:** *6 servings*

BLUEBERRY CREAM PIE

Who doesn't love pie? This pastry is heaped with fresh plump blueberries, sauced with spiced cream, and topped with crumb streusel. What's not to love?

CRUMB STREUSEL

¾ cup all-purpose flour
½ cup granulated sugar
8 tablespoons unsalted butter, cut into small pieces

FILLING

¼ cup all-purpose flour
⅔ cup granulated sugar
1 teaspoon ground cinnamon
½ teaspoon ground ginger
1 cup heavy or whipping cream
3 cups fresh blueberries, rinsed and drained
1 unbaked deep-dish 9-inch pie shell (Perfect Pie Pastry, page 92, ¼ recipe)

1. Preheat oven to 375°F. To catch drips, place baking sheet or a piece of aluminum foil on lower oven rack.

2. *Prepare streusel:* In a medium bowl, combine flour and sugar. With a wire pastry blender, cut in butter until mixture is crumbly. Set aside.

3. *Prepare filling:* In another medium bowl, thoroughly mix together flour, sugar, cinnamon, and ginger. Gradually add cream, whisking until blended.

4. Fill unbaked pie shell with blueberries. Pour filling over berries and top with streusel.

5. Bake in the middle of oven for 55 to 60 minutes or until center puffs up and top is evenly browned. Cover loosely with aluminum foil if top browns too quickly before center is set.

6. Remove from oven onto a wire rack and cool for at least 2 hours.

7. Cut into wedges. Serve warm or at room temperature with ice cream and a cup of coffee.

Cool remaining pie completely, cover, and refrigerate.

YIELD: *8 servings*

BUTTERMILK PIE

A pie angel brings Linda this creamy decadence each year for her birthday. For this, the best sugar pie ever, it's worth having another birthday.

NOTE

❏ *Pie may be served chilled.*

1½ cups granulated sugar
1 tablespoon cornstarch
8 tablespoons unsalted butter, melted and cooled
3 large eggs, lightly beaten
½ cup buttermilk
1 teaspoon pure vanilla extract

¼ cup sliced almonds
1 unbaked 9-inch pie shell (Perfect Pie Pastry, page 92, ¼ recipe)

1. Preheat oven to 325°F.

2. In a large bowl, sift together sugar and cornstarch. With an electric mixer set on medium-low speed, add melted butter, eggs, buttermilk, and vanilla and beat until blended. Do not beat filling to a frenzy.

3. Sprinkle bottom of unbaked pie shell with almonds. Pour filling into pie shell.

4. Bake in the middle of oven for 40 to 45 minutes or until crust is lightly golden, top is golden brown, and center of filling is almost set.

5. Remove from oven onto a wire rack and cool for at least 1 hour.

6. Cut into wedges. Serve warm or at room temperature with a cup of coffee.

Cool remaining pie completely, cover, and refrigerate.

YIELD: *8 servings*

COCONUT PECAN PIE

This nontraditional version of pecan pie uses a surprising combination of ingredients.

1   **cup granulated sugar**
8   **tablespoons unsalted butter, melted and cooled**
⅛   **teaspoon salt**
2   **large eggs, lightly beaten**
1   **tablespoon distilled white vinegar**
½   **cup lightly packed sweetened, shredded coconut**
½   **cup chopped pecans**
½   **cup raisins**
1   **unbaked 8-inch pie shell (Perfect Pie Pastry, page 92, ¼ recipe)**

1. Preheat oven to 325°F.

2. In a large bowl and with a sturdy wooden spoon, stir sugar, melted butter, salt, eggs, and vinegar until blended. Stir in coconut, pecans, and raisins.

3. Pour coconut filling into unbaked pie shell, distributing coconut, pecans, and raisins evenly.

4. Bake in the middle of oven for 40 minutes or until crust is lightly golden and top is golden brown.

5. Remove from oven onto a wire rack and cool for at least 1 hour.

6. Cut into wedges. Serve warm or at room temperature with a cup of coffee.

Cool remaining pie completely and cover.

YIELD: *6 servings*

CHOCOLATE MOUSSE TART

A toasted-almond pastry hugs mounds of Amaretto-flavored mousse. Earn a kiss with this chocolate bliss.

PASTRY

1¼ cups all-purpose flour

¾ cup sliced almonds, toasted in a 350°F oven for 6 to 8 minutes

¼ cup confectioners' sugar

⅛ teaspoon salt

12 tablespoons unsalted butter, cold, cut into tablespoons

2 large egg yolks

½ teaspoon pure almond extract

MOUSSE

8 ounces semisweet chocolate, chopped

4 ounces unsweetened chocolate, chopped

12 tablespoons unsalted butter, cut into tablespoons

5 large egg yolks, lightly beaten

3 tablespoons Amaretto or other almond-flavored liqueur

5 large egg whites, room temperature

⅛ teaspoon cream of tartar

¼ cup granulated sugar

1 cup heavy or whipping cream

⅓ cup sliced almonds, toasted in a 350°F oven for 6 to 8 minutes

1. *Prepare pastry:* In a food processor, place flour, almonds, confectioners' sugar, and salt and process with the steel blade until nuts are finely chopped, 15 seconds.

2. Add butter and process until coarse crumbs form. Add egg yolks and almond extract; pulse until dough forms.

3. Shape pastry dough into a smooth-sided disk, wrap in plastic wrap, and refrigerate for 1 hour.

4. Set aside an ungreased 9½-inch tart pan with a removable bottom. Preheat oven to 350°F.

5. Roll out dough between sheets of wax paper into a 12-inch circle. Remove top sheet of wax paper, turn dough into ungreased pan, and remove remaining wax paper. Gently work dough into bottom and sides of pan and trim excess dough.

6. Bake in the middle of oven for 20 minutes or until golden and pastry pulls away from sides of pan.

7. Remove from oven onto a wire rack and cool completely.

8. *Prepare mousse:* In the top of a double boiler over gently simmering water, melt chocolate and butter, stirring until smooth. Remove from heat and whisk first egg yolks, then Amaretto, into chocolate mixture.

9. In a clean, dry, large bowl and with an electric mixer set on medium-low speed, beat egg whites until foamy. Add cream of tartar and increase mixer speed to medium-high, beating until soft peaks form. Gradually add sugar, beating until stiff but not dry. With a rubber spatula, gently fold a third of the egg whites into chocolate mixture; fold in remaining egg whites.

10. In a large bowl and with an electric mixer set on medium speed, whip cream until peaks just begin to hold their shape. With the rubber spatula, gently fold whipped cream into chocolate mixture until mousse is uniform in color. Cover and refrigerate for 2 hours.

11. *Assemble tart:* Scoop large dollops of mousse into pastry and, with the back of a clean spoon or rubber spatula, swirl dollops to cover crust evenly. Refrigerate; cover with plastic wrap when filling is firm.

12. One hour before serving, remove tart from refrigerator. Carefully remove outer rim of tart pan and garnish tart with almonds.

13. Cut into wedges. Serve at room temperature with sweetened whipped cream and a cup of coffee.

Cover remaining tart and refrigerate.

YIELD: *10 servings*

VIENNESE ALMOND TART

Make this sophisticated shortbread in a second. Simply sensational, one serving is enough, maybe not.

1⅔ cups all-purpose flour
1½ cups granulated sugar
⅛ teaspoon salt
1   cup unsalted butter, melted and cooled
2   large eggs, lightly beaten
2   tablespoons pure almond extract
¾   cup sliced almonds

1. Brush a 9½-inch tart pan with a removable bottom with melted butter (this is *not* the 1 cup melted butter used later in the recipe). Dust lightly with flour. Preheat oven to 350°F.

2. In a large bowl, sift together flour, sugar, and salt. With an electric mixer set on medium-low speed, add 1 cup melted butter, eggs, and almond extract and beat until smooth.

3. Spread batter evenly into prepared pan. Sprinkle top with sliced almonds. With the back of a spoon or your fingertips, gently press almonds into batter.

4. Bake in the middle of oven for 35 minutes or until top is golden.

5. Remove from oven onto a wire rack and cool for at least 30 minutes. Carefully remove outer rim of tart pan.

6. Cut into wedges. Serve warm or at room temperature with a cup of coffee.

Cool remaining tart completely and cover.

YIELD: *20 (1-inch) wedges*

GINGERED PLUM CRISP

Savor the best of the season. When you see a plum, grab it, and enjoy this duo, sweet and tart, plain and fancy.

PLUM FILLING

6	tablespoons firmly packed light brown sugar
3	tablespoons all-purpose flour
½	teaspoon ground ginger
½	teaspoon ground cinnamon
7–9	firm purple plums, pitted and cut into eighths (4 cups)

TOPPING

1	cup all-purpose flour
1	cup granulated sugar
1	teaspoon baking powder
⅛	teaspoon salt
¼	teaspoon ground ginger
1	large egg, lightly beaten
8	tablespoons unsalted butter, melted

NOTES

❑ *For the cholesterol conscious, substitute margarine for butter.*
❑ *Indulge and top the crisp with vanilla ice cream or sweetened whipped cream, as much or as little as you like.*

1. Lightly butter a 1½-quart soufflé or deep-sided baking dish. Preheat oven to 375°F.

2. *Prepare filling:* In a large bowl, combine brown sugar, flour, ginger, and cinnamon. Add plums and, with a rubber spatula, toss gently to coat fruit.

3. Spoon filling into prepared dish. Set aside.

4. *Prepare topping:* In a medium bowl, sift together flour, granulated sugar, baking powder, salt, and ginger. Add egg and mix until crumbly.

5. Sprinkle topping evenly over filling. Slowly pour melted butter over topping, coating it well.

6. Bake in the middle of oven for 40 to 45 minutes or until top is golden brown and filling begins to bubble up through topping.

7. Remove from oven onto a wire rack and cool for 30 minutes.

8. Spoon into serving bowls. Serve warm with a cup of coffee.

Cool remaining crisp completely and cover.

YIELD: *6 servings*

WARM APPLE COBBLER

Cozy up with Flo Braker's simple pastry-topped apple cobbler. Flo is the author of *The Simple Art of Perfect Baking* and *Sweet Miniatures: The Art of Making Bite-Size Desserts.*

APPLE FILLING

4   tablespoons unsalted butter

6–8 apples (7 to 8 ounces each), preferably Granny Smith and/or Golden Delicious, peeled, cored, and cut into ¼-inch slices (approximately 8 slices per half)

½   cup granulated sugar

⅛   teaspoon ground cinnamon

1   tablespoon lemon juice

PASTRY

1¾ cups all-purpose flour

2   tablespoons granulated sugar

1   tablespoon baking powder

½   teaspoon salt

6   tablespoons unsalted butter, cut into small pieces

1   teaspoon finely grated orange zest

6   tablespoons heavy or whipping cream

2   tablespoons cold water

Heavy or whipping cream, enough to brush top of pastry

1   tablespoon granulated sugar for topping

1. Set aside a 9- by 14-inch oval au gratin dish or a 9- by 13-inch Pyrex baking dish.

2. *Prepare filling:* In a large heavy skillet over medium heat, melt butter. Add apples, sugar, and cinnamon and sauté until apples are tender, not soft, 8 to 10 minutes. Stir in lemon juice. Arrange apple mixture in baking dish. Let mixture cool for 20 to 30 minutes before preparing pastry dough.

3. Adjust oven rack to lower third of oven and preheat to 425°F.

4. *Prepare pastry:* In a large bowl, sift together flour, the 2 tablespoons sugar, baking powder, and salt. Cut in butter until the mixture resembles coarse meal. Stir in zest. Gradually add cream and then the water, mixing by hand until dough forms a cohesive ball.

5. On a lightly floured surface, roll out dough until slightly smaller than the dimensions of the baking dish.

6. Place pastry on top of apple filling. Brush top of pastry with enough cream and sprinkle with the 1 tablespoon sugar. Cut several slits or a small hole in the center of pastry to allow steam to escape.

7. Bake in the lower third of oven for 20 to 25 minutes or until pastry is golden and fruit is bubbly.

8. Remove from oven onto a wire rack.

9. Spoon into serving bowls. Serve warm with vanilla ice cream or frozen yogurt and a cup of coffee.

Cool remaining cobbler completely and cover.

YIELD: *10 servings*

COMPANY CAKES
AND TORTES

In one of the alpine regions of rural Salzburg, Austria, there is a saying around for almost everything. When it comes to coffee the elders would advise:

> *"Wennst g'sund willst bleib'n und lang willst leb'n*
> *must an Kaffee ein Wasser geb'n."*

If one would translate that literally:

> *"If you want to stay healthy and live a long life*
> *you must have a glass of water after your cup of coffee."*

In the fine cafés of Austria you still get a glass of water on your silver tray with your coffee. In the older cafés there are beautiful ornate spouts above a marble sink. The waiter (Herr Ober) will "pour" the water almost in front of your eyes.

There is a very interesting health and taste aspect to this: While coffee sometimes is thinned down to reduce the strength for various reasons, it is in this case diluted afterwards during digestion. This way the guest can enjoy the strength and flavor of the coffee.

After all, why would one want to drink a cup of coffee if it doesn't taste like one?

—Markus Färbinger, C.M.P.C., Senior Pastry Chef-Instructor of
The Culinary Institute of America in Hyde Park, New York

APPLE SPICE CAKE AND ORANGE BUTTERED RUM SAUCE

Simply scrumptious, serve this autumn-spiced dessert from Stephan Pyles, chef-owner of Star Canyon restaurant in Dallas, Texas.

Stephan begins, "Upon arising in the morning, I make my way to the kitchen, where the addictive fragrance of French Roast assures me that my automatically programmable coffee maker was a worthwhile investment.

"I pour the strong, black Java in the biggest cup I can find and take my usual seat on the deck overlooking my garden. As my morning ritual begins, I review the day ahead with great enthusiasm. Knowing how busy, hectic and frenzied the day will likely become, I refuse to rush this serene prelude. For one delightful hour, the world is at bay as I sit and contemplate with my perfectly brewed cup of liquid fortification."

NOTE

❏ *We serve Apple Spice Cake with Orange Buttered Rum Sauce (recipe follows), 2 tablespoons for each of 12 servings.*

2   cups all-purpose flour

1   cup cake flour

1½   teaspoons baking soda

½   teaspoon freshly grated nutmeg

½   teaspoon ground cinnamon

¼   teaspoon ground cloves

¼   teaspoon ground mace

¼   teaspoon ground ginger

1½   cups butter, room temperature, cut into tablespoons

2   cups granulated sugar

3   large eggs

3½   cups unpeeled tart green apples, cored and cut into ¼-inch dice

1¾   cups chopped pecans, roasted in a 350°F oven for 7 to 10 minutes

1. Butter and lightly flour a 10-inch springform pan. Preheat oven to 325°F.

2. Sift together all-purpose flour, cake flour, baking soda, nutmeg, cinnamon, cloves, mace, and ginger. Set aside.

3. In a large bowl and with an electric mixer set on medium speed, cream together butter and sugar until light and fluffy. Add eggs, one at a time, beating well after each addition.

4. With a rubber spatula, gradually fold flour mixture into butter mixture until thoroughly combined. Add apples and pecans, blending well with the spatula.

5. Spread batter evenly into prepared pan.

6. Bake in the middle of oven for 1 hour and 30 minutes to 1 hour and 45 minutes or until a paring knife inserted in center comes out clean.

7. Remove from oven onto a wire rack and cool completely.

8. To loosen rim of springform pan, run a sharp knife along edge of cake. Remove rim. Run the knife along bottom of cake and carefully transfer onto a serving plate.

9. Cut into slices. Serve at room temperature with ice cream, caramel sauce, and a cup of coffee.

Cover remaining cake.

YIELD: *12 to 16 servings*

ORANGE BUTTERED RUM SAUCE
1   **cup firmly packed light brown sugar**
1   **tablespoon all-purpose flour**
1   **large egg, lightly beaten**
¼   **cup dark rum**
¼   **cup fresh orange juice**
4   **tablespoons unsalted butter, cut into tablespoons**

NOTE

❑ *Sauce may be refrigerated for up to 10 days and can be reheated in the top of a double boiler.*

1. Combine all ingredients in the top of a double boiler. Over gently simmering water, cook, stirring continuously, until sauce thickens slightly. Do not boil. If the mixture gets hotter than 185°F, it will curdle.

2. Remove from heat and, with a fine-mesh sieve, strain into a serving bowl.

3. Serve warm.

Cool remaining sauce completely, cover, and refrigerate.

YIELD: *scant 1½ cups*

BANANA CHIFFON CAKE WITH VANILLA WHIPPED CREAM

This cake is a sister to angel food; a dressy dessert that is heavenly light, inside and out.

NOTES

❑ *The egg whites should be at room temperature and free from contaminants and specks of egg yolk.*
❑ *When whipping cream, use cold heavy or whipping cream, a chilled bowl, and chilled beaters for best results.*
❑ *Brush crumbs from cake before frosting.*
❑ *When frosting cake, remember to frost the inside edge.*

C A K E

2¼ cups sifted cake flour
1½ cups granulated sugar
1 tablespoon baking powder
½ teaspoon salt
½ cup vegetable oil
5 large egg yolks
⅓ cup cold water
1 cup well-mashed very ripe bananas (3 medium)
1 teaspoon pure vanilla extract
8 large egg whites, room temperature
½ teaspoon cream of tartar

V A N I L L A   W H I P P E D   C R E A M

1½ cups heavy or whipping cream
3 tablespoons granulated sugar
1 teaspoon pure vanilla extract

½ cup coarsely chopped pecans, toasted in a 350°F oven for 7 to 10 minutes

1. Set aside an ungreased 10-inch tube pan, preferably with a removable bottom. Preheat oven to 325°F.

2. In a large bowl, sift together sifted cake flour, sugar, baking powder, and salt. Make a well in dry ingredients and add in order, without beating, oil, egg yolks, cold water, mashed bananas, and vanilla. With an electric mixer set on medium-low speed, beat until thoroughly combined.

3. In a clean, dry, large bowl and with an electric mixer set on medium-low speed, beat egg whites until foamy. Increase mixer speed to medium-high and add cream of tartar, beating continuously until stiff. Beat 1 minute more. With a rubber spatula, gently fold a third of the egg whites into batter; fold in remaining egg whites.

4. Pour batter into ungreased pan and, with the rubber spatula, gently smooth top.

5. Bake in the middle of oven for 50 to 55 minutes or until top springs back when touched lightly.

6. Remove from oven and immediately invert onto a heatproof funnel or bottle. Cool completely.

7. To remove from pan, run a sharp knife along outside and inside edges of cake. Carefully invert onto a serving plate. If pan has a removable bottom, run knife along bottom of cake. If not using within the hour, wrap cake with plastic wrap.

8. One hour before serving, *prepare Vanilla Whipped Cream:* In a large bowl and with an electric mixer set on medium speed, whip cream, sugar, and vanilla until soft peaks form and cream is just firm enough to frost the cake.

9. Spread Vanilla Whipped Cream evenly on sides and top of cake. Top with pecans.

10. Cut into slices. Serve at room temperature with a cup of coffee.

Cover remaining cake and refrigerate.

YIELD: *12 servings*

COFFEE ANGEL FOOD CAKE WITH COFFEE ALMOND GLAZE

Sinless and celestial—oh, it's so good. The Coffee Almond Glaze is all that's needed to reach the golden gate.

CAKE

4	teaspoons instant espresso coffee powder
1	cup sifted cake flour
½	cup granulated sugar
12	large egg whites, room temperature
½	teaspoon salt
2	tablespoons plus 1½ teaspoons cold water
1½	teaspoons cream of tartar
½	teaspoon pure almond extract
½	teaspoon pure vanilla extract
1	cup granulated sugar

COFFEE ALMOND GLAZE

2½	tablespoons unsalted butter, room temperature, cut into tablespoons
1	cup confectioners' sugar, sifted
½	teaspoon instant espresso coffee powder, dissolved in 2 tablespoons plus 1½ teaspoons hot water
¼	teaspoon pure almond extract
¼	teaspoon pure vanilla extract

1. Set aside an ungreased 10-inch tube pan. Preheat oven to 375°F.

2. With a mortar and pestle, pulverize coffee powder for a few seconds.

3. Sift together, 6 times, sifted cake flour, the ½ cup sugar, and espresso powder. Set aside.

4. In a clean, dry, large bowl and with an electric mixer set on medium-low speed, beat egg whites and salt until foamy. Increase mixer speed to medium-high, add water, cream of tartar, almond extract, and vanilla extract, beating continuously until stiff but not dry. Gradually add the 1 cup granulated sugar, 2 tablespoons at a time, beating continuously until sugar is incorporated.

5. Sift a small amount of the sifted flour mixture over whites and, with a rubber spatula, fold in gently. Continue until all the flour mixture is incorporated and no pockets of flour remain.

6. Pour batter into ungreased tube pan and, with the back of the rubber spatula, gently smooth top. With a knife, cut through batter to break up air bubbles.

7. Bake in the middle of oven for 30 to 35 minutes or until top is browned. Do not overbake. Turn off oven and leave cake in oven for an additional 5 minutes.

8. Remove from oven and immediately invert onto a heatproof funnel or bottle. Cool completely.

9. To remove from pan, run a sharp knife along outside and inside edges of cake. Carefully invert onto a serving plate. If pan has a removable bottom, run knife along bottom of cake.

10. *Prepare Coffee Almond Glaze:* In a large bowl and with a hand-held electric mixer set on low speed, cream together butter and sifted confectioners' sugar. Add espresso coffee, almond extract, and vanilla extract. Increase mixer speed to medium and beat until smooth.

11. Spoon glaze over top of cake.

12. Cut into slices. Serve at room temperature with a cup of coffee.

Cover remaining cake.

YIELD: *12 servings*

ITALIAN CREAM CAKE WITH RASPBERRY FILLING

Espresso yourself. Prepare for a smashing success when you create this gorgeous torte-like dessert. Full of sweet coconut and toasted pecans, this triple-layered cake has a spiked berry filling and rich cream cheese frosting.

NOTES

❏ *The egg whites should be at room temperature and free from contaminants and specks of egg yolk.*
❏ *If oven space is limited, position racks in middle and upper half of oven. Rotate pans halfway through baking, allowing cake layers to bake evenly.*
❏ *Brush crumbs from cake before assembling.*
❏ *Filling may be thinned with an additional tablespoon of Kirschwasser.*

CAKE

2	cups all-purpose flour
1	teaspoon baking soda
1/2	teaspoon salt
1 1/2	cups solid shortening
8	tablespoons unsalted butter, room temperature, cut into tablespoons
2	cups granulated sugar
5	large egg yolks
1	cup buttermilk
1	tablespoon pure vanilla extract
2	cups sweetened, shredded coconut
1	cup coarsely chopped pecans, toasted in a 350°F oven for 7 to 10 minutes
5	large egg whites, room temperature

CREAM CHEESE FROSTING

1	8-ounce package cream cheese, room temperature
8	tablespoons unsalted butter, room temperature, cut into tablespoons
1	1-pound box (4 1/2 cups) confectioners' sugar, sifted
1	teaspoon pure vanilla extract
1	tablespoon Kirschwasser or other cherry-flavored brandy

RASPBERRY FILLING

1/2	cup seedless raspberry preserves
1	tablespoon Kirschwasser or other cherry-flavored brandy

1. Grease three 9-inch cake pans. Line bottoms of cake pans with wax or parchment paper; grease paper. Dust lightly with flour. Preheat oven to 350°F.

2. Sift together flour, baking soda, and salt. Set aside.

3. In a large bowl and with an electric mixer set on medium speed, cream together shortening, butter, and sugar until light and fluffy. Add egg yolks, one at a time, beating well after each addition. Add buttermilk and vanilla and beat until thoroughly combined. Stop mixer and scrape down bottom and sides of bowl as necessary.

4. Set mixer on low speed. Gradually add flour mixture, beating until just incorporated. Mix in coconut and pecans.

5. In a clean, dry, large bowl and with an electric mixer set on medium-low speed, beat egg whites until foamy. Increase mixer speed to medium-high; beat continuously until stiff but not dry. With a rubber spatula, gently fold a third of the egg whites into batter; fold in remaining egg whites.

6. Pour equal portions of batter into prepared pans and, with the back of the rubber spatula, smooth tops.

7. Bake in the middle of oven for 30 minutes or until toothpick inserted in center comes out clean. Do not overbake.

8. Remove from oven onto a wire rack and cool in pans for 10 minutes.

9. To remove from pans, run a sharp knife along outside edge of cake layers. Carefully invert onto wire rack and cool completely, 2 hours.

10. *Prepare frosting:* In a large bowl and with an electric mixer set on medium speed, beat cream cheese and butter until smooth. Reduce mixer speed to low. Gradually add sifted confectioners' sugar and beat until creamy. Stop mixer and scrape down bottom and sides of bowl as necessary. Beat in vanilla and Kirschwasser. Set aside.

11. *Prepare Raspberry Filling:* In a small heavy saucepan over low heat, heat raspberry preserves until melted. Remove from heat and stir in Kirschwasser.

12. *Assemble cake:* Place bottom cake layer on serving plate and spread evenly with ½ cup frosting. Add middle layer; spread evenly with warm Raspberry Filling. Add top layer; spread top and side of cake evenly with remaining frosting. If not using immediately, refrigerate.

13. Cut into slices. Serve at room temperature with a cup of coffee.

Cover remaining cake and refrigerate.

YIELD: *12 servings*

LA MAXINE

Linda and Barbara had been making this flourless chocolate cake for years, years before they met. This coffee-seasoned cake was developed by Bert Greene, the late food writer and television personality. Coffee brings people together, and chocolate doesn't hurt.

NOTES

❑ *We used Medaglia D'Oro Instant Espresso Coffee powder.*
❑ *We used a food processor to grind the walnuts for the cake: Be careful not to overprocess.*
❑ *The egg whites should be at room temperature and free from contaminants and specks of egg yolk.*
❑ *We feel this cake is wonderful with just the icing.*
❑ *Emily Hegeman Cavanagh wouldn't think of celebrating her birthday without this.*

C A K E

1½ cups granulated sugar
⅓ cup water
1½ teaspoons instant espresso coffee powder
1½ cups (9 ounces) semisweet chocolate morsels
1½ teaspoons pure vanilla extract
9 tablespoons unsalted butter, room temperature
12 large egg yolks
1½ cups finely ground walnuts
3 tablespoons fine dry bread crumbs
12 large egg whites, room temperature
¼ teaspoon salt

C O F F E E - C H O C O L A T E   I C I N G

1⅓ cups semisweet chocolate morsels
⅓ cup water
4 teaspoons instant espresso coffee powder
1 cup plus 2 tablespoons unsalted butter, room temperature, cut into tablespoons
3 large egg yolks
1 cup confectioners' sugar

C H O C O L A T E   T R I A N G L E S

1 cup semisweet chocolate morsels
2 teaspoons vegetable shortening, divided
2 teaspoons instant espresso coffee powder, divided
1 cup milk chocolate morsels

1½ cups chopped walnuts

1. Butter two 9-inch cake pans. Line bottoms of cake pans with wax or parchment paper; butter paper. Dust lightly with flour. Preheat oven to 350°F.

2. In a small heavy saucepan over low heat, heat sugar, water, and

114

espresso powder, stirring constantly until warm, 5 minutes. Add semi-sweet chocolate morsels and vanilla, stirring constantly until chocolate is melted and mixture is smooth. Remove from heat and cool for 5 minutes.

3. In a large bowl and with an electric mixer set on medium speed, cream butter. Add egg yolks, one at a time, beating well after each addition. Gradually add melted chocolate mixture, walnuts, and bread crumbs and beat for 3 minutes.

4. In a clean, dry, large bowl and with an electric mixer set on medium-high speed, beat egg whites and salt until stiff but not dry. With a rubber spatula, gently fold a third of egg whites into chocolate mixture; fold in remaining whites.

5. Pour equal portions of batter into prepared pans.

6. Bake in the middle of oven for 50 to 60 minutes or until toothpick inserted in center comes out clean.

7. Remove from oven onto a wire rack and cool in pans for 15 minutes. Remove cakes from pans onto wire rack and cool completely, 2 hours. Cake will settle as it cools.

8. *Prepare icing:* In a small heavy saucepan over low heat, heat semisweet chocolate morsels, water, and espresso powder, stirring constantly until chocolate is melted, 5 minutes. Remove from heat and refrigerate until cold, 20 minutes.

9. In a large bowl and with an electric mixer set on medium speed, cream butter. Add egg yolks, one at a time, beating well after each addition.

10. Reduce mixer speed to low. Gradually beat in first confectioners' sugar, then the cold chocolate mixture. Stop mixer and scrape down bottom and sides of bowl as necessary. Set aside or refrigerate until firm enough to spread.

11. *Prepare chocolate triangles:* Line baking sheet with aluminum foil. In the top of a double boiler over gently simmering water, melt semisweet chocolate morsels, 1 teaspoon of the 2 teaspoons vegetable shortening, and 1 teaspoon of the 2 teaspoons espresso powder, stirring until smooth. Pour melted chocolate mixture onto one side of prepared baking sheet and, with a metal spatula, smooth to make a 6- by 5- by ½-inch rectangle. Refrigerate. Repeat with milk chocolate, remaining 1 teaspoon shortening, and remaining 1 teaspoon coffee powder. Pour onto remaining side of baking sheet and smooth to make another 6- by 5- by ½-inch rectangle. Refrigerate until firm.

12. Remove chocolate rectangles from refrigerator. Let stand at room temperature for about 2 minutes. With a sharp thin-bladed knife, cut each chocolate rectangle in half crosswise, then lengthwise into quarters to make 8 small rectangles. Cut each small rectangle in half diagonally to make 16 triangles. Refrigerate if needed to reform.

13. *Assemble cake:* This cake is very moist and delicate; handle gently while assembling. Place bottom cake layer on serving plate and spread evenly with ½ cup icing. Top with remaining layer; spread top and side of cake evenly with 1½ cups of the icing. Press chopped walnuts onto side of cake. Fit pastry bag with star tip. Spoon remaining icing into pastry bag; pipe in ring on top of cake. Place chocolate triangles, alternating between light and dark, in a circle on top of cake. Press remaining triangles, alternating between light and dark, into side of cake. Refrigerate.

14. One hour before serving, remove cake from refrigerator.

15. Cut into slices. Serve at room temperature with a cup of coffee.

Cover remaining cake and refrigerate.

YIELD: *12 servings*

DELUXE POUND CAKE

This homemade pound cake is hard to beat. Serve it plain or dressed, with fresh fruit or cream, iced or whipped. Sober or sauced, it has as many uses as the basic black dress.

1   **cup butter, room temperature, cut into tablespoons**
3   **cups granulated sugar**
6   **large eggs**
3   **cups sifted all-purpose flour**
2   **teaspoons pure vanilla extract**
1   **cup heavy or whipping cream**

1. Generously grease a 12-cup Bundt pan or 10-inch tube pan.
2. In a large bowl and with an electric mixer set on medium speed, cream together butter and sugar for 10 minutes. Add eggs, one at a time, beating well after each addition. Stop mixer and scrape down bottom and sides of bowl as necessary.
3. Set mixer on low speed. Gradually add flour, beating until just incorporated. Beat in vanilla. Add cream and beat until blended.
4. Spread batter evenly into prepared pan.
5. Place in the middle of a cold oven. Set oven temperature at 325°F and bake for 1 hour and 25 minutes or until cake tester inserted in center comes out clean.
6. Remove from oven onto a wire rack and cool completely, 2 hours.
7. To remove from pan, run a sharp knife along outside and inside edges of cake. Carefully invert onto a serving plate.
8. Cut into slices. Serve at room temperature with a cup of coffee.

Cover remaining cake.

YIELD: *12 servings*

RUM RAISIN CHEESECAKE

This real adult treat pleases the most critical of cheesecake lovers. For relaxing entertainment, make this true gem days ahead.

NOTES

❏ *Raisins will settle in the bottom of pan.*
❏ *If you wish to remove bottom of springform pan before serving, freeze cheesecake. When frozen, run a sharp knife along bottom of crust and carefully remove bottom of pan. Rewrap if freezing, or transfer onto a serving plate and refrigerate.*
❏ *This cheesecake reaches its peak of flavor 24 to 48 hours after preparation.*

1¼ cups raisins
½ cup dark rum

CRUST
1 cup graham cracker crumbs (7 whole crackers)
2 tablespoons granulated sugar
2 tablespoons ground walnuts
4 tablespoons unsalted butter, melted

CREAM CHEESE FILLING
5 8-ounce packages cream cheese, room temperature
1½ cups granulated sugar
1 tablespoon pure vanilla extract
5 large eggs
3 large egg yolks
⅓ cup heavy or whipping cream

1. Lightly grease a 10-inch springform pan. Cover outside of springform pan with aluminum foil to prevent leakage of filling from seam. Preheat oven to 325°F.

2. Soak raisins in rum for at least 30 minutes.

3. *Prepare crust:* In a medium bowl, combine graham cracker crumbs, sugar, .walnuts, and melted butter. Press crumb mixture into bottom of prepared pan. Bake in the middle of oven for 7 to 8 minutes or until lightly browned. Remove from oven onto a wire rack and cool for 10 minutes. Maintain oven temperature.

4. *Prepare filling*: In a large bowl and with an electric mixer set on medium-low speed, beat cream cheese until smooth. Beat in sugar and vanilla. Stop mixer and scrape down bottom and sides of bowl as necessary. Add eggs and egg yolks, one at a time, beating well after each addition. Beat in rum-raisin mixture and cream until well blended. Pour filling over crust, distributing raisins evenly.

5. Bake in the middle of oven for 1 hour. Only the edge of the cake will be firm. Turn off oven and leave in oven for an additional 30 minutes. The center of the cake will firm during this period.

6. Remove from oven onto a wire rack and cool completely, 4 or

5 hours. Remove foil from outside of pan. Cover with plastic wrap and refrigerate in pan overnight.

7. To remove rim of springform pan, run a sharp knife along edge of cake.

8. Cut into slices. Serve chilled with a cup of coffee.

Cover remaining cake and refrigerate.

YIELD: *16 servings*

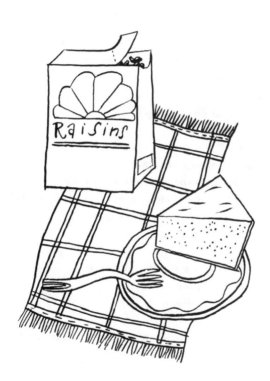

DEEP DARK CHOCOLATE TORTE

A sugared nut crust, deep chocolate fudge, and an espresso-flavored chocolate mousse make for a show-stopping dessert. It's made in stages for easy preparation.

PECAN CRUST

2½ cups finely chopped pecans, toasted in a 350°F oven for 6 to 8 minutes

½ cup granulated sugar

¼ teaspoon salt

8 tablespoons unsalted butter, melted

BITTERSWEET CHOCOLATE GANACHE

8 ounces bittersweet (not unsweetened) chocolate, chopped

4 tablespoons unsalted butter

1 cup heavy or whipping cream

2 tablespoons light corn syrup

CHOCOLATE COFFEE MOUSSE

2 ounces unsweetened chocolate, chopped

1 tablespoon instant espresso coffee powder

1 cup unsalted butter, room temperature, cut into tablespoons

1½ cups firmly packed dark brown sugar

4 large eggs, room temperature

SWEETENED WHIPPED CREAM

1 cup heavy or whipping cream

¼ cup confectioners' sugar

Shaved bittersweet chocolate, enough to garnish top

1. Set aside an ungreased 9-inch springform pan. Preheat oven to 350°F.

2. *Prepare crust:* In a medium bowl, combine pecans, sugar, and salt. Add melted butter and combine. Firmly press pecan mixture into bottom of pan. Freeze crust until firm, 10 minutes.

3. Cover outside of springform pan with aluminum foil to prevent leakage from seam. Bake in the middle of oven for 15 minutes.

4. Remove from oven onto a wire rack and cool completely. Remove foil, cover pan with plastic wrap, and refrigerate until firm.

5. *Prepare ganache:* In the top of a double boiler over gently simmering water, melt bittersweet chocolate and butter, stirring until smooth. Remove from heat and gradually stir in first cream, then corn syrup. Stir occasionally until thick and completely cool. Spread ganache evenly over chilled crust. Cover and refrigerate until firm.

6. *Prepare mousse:* In the top of a double boiler over gently simmering water, melt unsweetened chocolate and espresso powder, stirring until smooth. Remove from heat.

7. In a large bowl and with an electric mixer set on medium speed, cream together butter and brown sugar until light and fluffy. Add eggs, one at a time, beating well after each addition. Stop mixer and scrape down bottom and sides of bowl as necessary.

8. Set mixer on low speed. Gradually add melted chocolate mixture and beat until smooth.

9. Spread mousse evenly over chilled ganache and crust. Cover and freeze several hours or overnight.

10. One hour before serving, remove from freezer. To remove rim of springform pan, run a sharp knife along edge of torte. Then run the knife along bottom of torte. Carefully transfer onto a serving plate and refrigerate.

11. *Prepare sweetened whipped cream:* In a large bowl and with an electric mixer set on medium speed, whip cream and confectioners' sugar until soft peaks form.

12. Cut into slices. Serve chilled with sweetened whipped cream, shaved bittersweet chocolate, and a cup of coffee.

Cover remaining torte and refrigerate or freeze.

YIELD: *12 servings*

ORANGE ALMOND TORTE

NOTES

❑ *To make orange confit, boil the peel of 4 oranges twice, changing water each time. Combine 1¾ cups granulated sugar, 1 cup water, and 2 tablespoons light corn syrup in a heavy medium saucepan. Add the orange peel and cook below simmer for 2 hours. Remove peel from syrup and finely dice. This makes 1 cup finely diced orange confit, enough for 2 tortes. Orange confit may be prepared ahead if kept in the syrup.*
❑ *We found the cake simple to prepare and worth the time to make the fresh orange confit. Candied orange peel may be substituted for orange confit.*
❑ *Torte may be prepared a day ahead and glazed before serving. Glazing under the broiler does not heat the torte significantly.*

This jam-glazed torte was developed by Markus Färbinger, C.M.P.C., senior pastry chef-instructor at The Culinary Institute of America in Hyde Park, New York.

"The cake stays unbelievably moist without being gooey or dense," Chef Färbinger assures. "The orange zest and the confit add a wonderful hint of flowery-bitterness that pairs well with a robust coffee. Serve this cake with a spoon of whipped heavy cream from a local farm."

16 ounces almond paste, cut into small pieces
12 large egg yolks, divided
2 large egg whites, room temperature
4 tablespoons fresh orange juice
5 teaspoons finely grated orange zest (4 oranges)
½ cup orange confit, finely diced (see notes)
6 large egg whites, room temperature
½ cup plus 1 tablespoon granulated sugar
½ cup cornstarch
8 tablespoons unsalted butter, melted
Sliced almonds, enough to sprinkle in pan and on finished torte
Orange jam, melted, enough to glaze finished torte
Confectioners' sugar, enough to dust finished torte

1. Butter a 10-inch round cake pan with 2-inch sides and sprinkle with some of the sliced almonds. Preheat oven to 350°F.

2. In a large bowl and with an electric mixer set on low speed, blend almond paste and 6 of the 12 egg yolks until almond paste is softened. Add remaining 6 egg yolks, the 2 egg whites, orange juice, zest, and confit and cream lightly until smooth. Do not whip or mixture will deflate during baking.

3. In a clean, dry, large bowl and with an electric mixer set on medium-low speed, beat the 6 egg whites until foamy. Increase mixer speed to medium-high and gradually add the sugar, beating continuously until soft peaks form. With a rubber spatula, gently fold beaten egg white mixture into almond paste mixture. Fold in first cornstarch and then melted butter.

4. Pour batter into prepared pan and, with the rubber spatula, gently smooth top.

5. Bake in the middle of oven for 45 minutes or until toothpick inserted in center comes out clean.

6. Remove from oven, run a sharp knife along edge of cake, and carefully invert onto a wire rack. Cool completely.

7. Glaze torte with melted orange jam, sprinkle with additional sliced almonds, and sift confectioners' sugar over top. Place torte on a baking sheet and lightly brown under broiler.

8. Transfer torte onto a serving plate and cut into slices. Serve at room temperature with a cup of coffee.

Cover remaining torte.

YIELD: *16 servings*

❏ *Use best-quality orange marmalade to glaze torte, or serve the cake without the glaze.*
❏ *The egg whites should be at room temperature and free of contaminants and specks of egg yolk.*

MORE COFFEE DELIGHTS

Fabulous coffee is one of the distinct pleasures of my life. I start every day with a cappuccino or two and continue sipping on them throughout the day. No matter what town I may be in I go out of my way to search out superior coffee—Starbucks, Spinelli, Café La Sameuse, or Illy Café—and I make sure that both my home and my restaurant are stocked with only the best as well. The machine is important, too. I realize that everyone cannot own a commercial espresso machine, but one should purchase the best machine possible. There is nothing worse than burnt, bitter coffee.

—Charlie H. Trotter, Chef-Proprietor of Charlie Trotter's restaurant in Chicago, Illinois, and Las Vegas, Nevada, and author of *Charlie Trotter's*

BEEF STEW WITH COFFEE

Charlie Trotter, chef-proprietor of Charlie Trotter's restaurant in Chicago, Illinois, and Las Vegas, Nevada, and author of *Charlie Trotter's*, turns conventional stew into an out-of-the-ordinary entrée with the addition of coffee, curry, and mango.

Chef Trotter confirms, "Cooking with coffee is interesting, too. It adds a subtle richness and a distinct flavor to both sweet and savory dishes. I use it in ice creams, chocolate desserts, and to flavor lamb, beef, or game. My 'Beef Stew with Coffee' is a perfect example of how coffee changes the character of something as simple as beef stew, adding a complexity and depth that is usually lacking."

½   **cup uncooked bacon**
1½ **pounds lean top round, cut into small cubes**
    Salt and pepper
½   **cup diced green bell pepper**
1   **cup diced carrots**
½   **cup diced celery**
18 **pearl onions, peeled**
1   **cup veal or chicken stock**
1½ **cups seeded, diced tomato**
¾   **cup strong coffee**
1   **teaspoon Worcestershire sauce**
1   **tablespoon stone-ground mustard**
1   **teaspoon paprika**
1   **teaspoon curry powder**
⅔   **cup cooked green peas**
⅓   **cup diced mango**

1. Set aside a 2-quart shallow baking dish. Preheat oven to 375°F.

2. In a large heavy skillet over low heat, render fat from bacon. With a slotted spoon, remove bacon from skillet and set aside.

3. Increase heat to medium and brown beef in the bacon fat; season lightly with salt and pepper.

4. Place bacon, beef, bell pepper, carrots, celery, and pearl onions in baking dish.

5. In the skillet used to brown the meat, put stock, tomato, coffee, Worcestershire sauce, mustard, paprika, and curry and boil for 3 to 4 minutes, whisking several times along the way. Season to taste with salt and pepper. Pour stock mixture into baking dish and cover.

  6. Bake for 2 hours or until meat is tender.

  7. Remove from oven. Stir in peas and mango and serve.

Cool remaining stew completely and refrigerate.

YIELD: *6 servings*

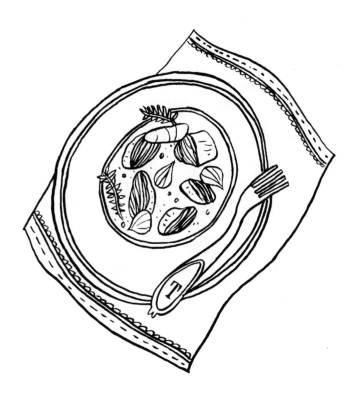

COUNTRY HAM AND RED EYE GRAVY

Scott Peacock, chef of Horseradish Grill in Atlanta, Georgia, and co-founder of The Society for the Revival and Preservation of Southern Food, suggests serving the ham with biscuits, grits, and eggs. "Make sure," Scott instructs, "to spoon gravy over ham and grits."

NOTE

❏ *We used 2 pounds of ham steak.*

6   **center-cut country ham steaks, ⅓ inch thick**
2   **tablespoons unsalted butter**
2½ **cups freshly brewed coffee**

1. With a cook's knife, carefully scrape both sides of each ham steak to remove any residual bone dust or particles left from slicing.

2. In a large nonreactive sauté pan or a cast-iron skillet, heat butter until hot and foaming. Over high heat, very quickly sauté each steak for about 1 minute a side. Remove steaks and set aside.

3. Pour off all but 1 tablespoon fat from the pan. Return pan to heat and add coffee. With a wooden spoon, stir to dislodge all bits and pieces stuck to the bottom of pan.

4. Return ham steaks to pan, cover tightly, and gently simmer in gravy for 20 to 30 minutes.

5. Serve hot with biscuits, grits, and eggs.

Cool remaining ham and refrigerate.

YIELD: *6 servings*

CBA COFFEE DRINK

"Moose's serves this warming coffee drink to a democratic mix of customers," states restaurant co-owner Mary Etta Moose in San Francisco, California.

"My father's first act of the day," Mary Etta recalls, "was making a pot of coffee, the aroma wafting through our home like a bugler, calling us from our beds. Today, in my San Francisco home in North Beach, the air, filled with scents from our three native coffee roasters, still harks me back to the first breakfast at which Daddy filled my mug with hot milk, and marked it with my first taste of coffee."

1   **raw sugar cube**
3   **ounces fresh hot coffee**
1   **jigger brandy**
1   **tablespoon Anisette liqueur**

1. In a warm 4-ounce footed glass, crush raw sugar cube in hot coffee.
2. Add brandy and stir.
3. Pour Anisette to float on top of the drink.

YIELD: *1 serving*

ORANGE ESPRESSO CHOCOLATE CHIP ICE CREAM

Not your average scoop, this flavor-infused ice cream was created by Jerry Tewell, pastry chef of Square One restaurant, San Francisco, California.

Jerry admits, "I'm glad I live in San Francisco where it's impossible to get a bad cappuccino."

4   cups heavy or whipping cream
1   cup granulated sugar
    Grated zest of 2 oranges
5   ounces (2 cups) espresso beans
9   large egg yolks
1½ teaspoons pure vanilla extract
    Pinch of salt
    Grand Marnier (orange-flavored liqueur) or Kahlúa (coffee-flavored liqueur), enough to balance the flavor of the custard, about 1 tablespoon
4   ounces bittersweet (not unsweetened) chocolate, chopped (¾ cup)

1. In a large heavy saucepan, combine cream and sugar. Over medium heat, bring cream mixture almost to a boil.

2. Remove from heat and stir in zest. Cover pan and steep for 10 minutes.

3. Stir in espresso beans. Cover and steep for at least 2 hours.

4. With a fine-mesh sieve or chinois, strain cream mixture and discard zest and beans. Return strained cream mixture to pan and reheat.

5. Temper egg yolks: In a small bowl, whisk yolks. Gradually add ½ cup hot cream mixture, whisking continuously. Whisk tempered yolks into remaining hot cream mixture. Cook slowly over low heat, stirring constantly, until custard is thick enough to coat the back of a spoon. Do not let the mixture boil. If the custard gets hotter than 185°F, it will curdle. Remove from heat.

6. With the fine-mesh sieve or chinois, strain custard into a large bowl. Stir in vanilla and salt. Place bowl in ice bath until custard is cold.

7. Taste custard. There should be a balance of the orange and coffee flavors. To bring up the flavor, stir in either Grand Marnier or

Kahlúa, a teaspoon at a time. If too much alcohol is added, the ice cream will not freeze sufficiently.

8. Cover and refrigerate overnight.

9. Fold chopped chocolate into custard. Pour custard into ice cream maker and follow manufacturer's directions. Scrape ice cream into freezer container and freeze.

10. Serve with a cup of coffee.

YIELD: *1 quart*

MAIL-ORDER SOURCES

BASSE'S CHOICE PLANTATION, LTD.
P.O. Box 1
Smithfield, Virginia 23430
(800) 292–2773
(Genuine Smithfield hams)

DEAN & DELUCA
560 Broadway
New York, New York 10012
(212) 431–1691
(Good-quality chocolate, including Valrhôna and Callebaut, and
Medaglia D'Oro Instant Espresso Coffee)

DILLMAN FARM
4955 West State Road 45
Bloomington, Indiana 47403
(812) 825–5525
FAX: (812) 825–4650
(Frozen persimmon pulp and best-quality preserves)

THE KING ARTHUR FLOUR BAKER'S CATALOGUE
P.O. Box 876
Norwich, Vermont 05055–0876
(800) 827–6836
FAX: (802) 649–5359
(Baking supplies and ingredients, including maple sugar and
extracts)

SWEET CELEBRATIONS
7009 Washington Avenue South
Edina, Minnesota 55439
(800) 328–6722
(Good-quality chocolate, including Lindt, Callebaut, and Merckens')

PENZEYS' SPICE HOUSE, LTD.
P.O. Box 1633
Milwaukee, Wisconsin 53201
(414) 574–0277
(Good-quality spices and extracts)

WOLF COFFEE COMPANY
1810 Mendocino Avenue
Santa Rosa, California 95401
(707) 524–8038
FAX: (707) 524–8040
(Coffee beans)

ZINFANDEL
59 West Grand Avenue
Chicago, Illinois 60610
(312) 257–1818
(Maple sugar)

The above mail-order sources, addresses, phone, and FAX numbers are correct upon submission of manuscript.

INDEX